YOUR BABY'S FIRST YEAR

Your Baby's First Year

Spiritual Reflections on Infant Development

Ruth Ann Parish, M.D.

Harold Shaw Publishers
Wheaton, Illinois

Unless otherwise indicated, all Scripture quotations are taken from the HOLY BIBLE: NEW INTERNATIONAL VERSION ®. NIV ®. Copyright © 1973, 1978, 1984 by International Bible Society. Used by permission of Zondervan Publishing House. All rights reserved.

Scripture quotations marked NRSV are taken from The New Revised Standard Version of the Bible, copyrighted 1989 by the Division of Christian Education of the National Council of the Churches of Christ in the United States of America, and are used by permission. All rights reserved.

Scripture quotations marked NLT are taken from the *Holy Bible,* New Living Translation, copyright © 1996. Used by permission of Tyndale House Publishers, Inc., Wheaton, Illinois 60189. All rights reserved.

Scripture quotations taken from the *King James Version* of the Bible are marked KJV.

ISBN 0-87788-560-5

Edited by Elizabeth Cody Newenhuyse

Photos © 1997 William Koechling

Cover and inside design by David LaPlaca

Library of Congress Cataloging-in-Publication Data

Parish, Ruth Ann, 1951-
    Your baby's first year : spiritual reflections on infant development /
    Ruth Ann Parish.
      p.   cm.
    ISBN 0-87788-560-5
    1. Parents—Religious life. 2. Infants—Development. 3. Parenting—
Religious aspects—Christianity. I. Title
BV4845.P37 1997
155.42'2—dc21   96-50943
                                       CIP

---

02 01 00 99 98

10 9 8 7 6 5 4 3 2

To

KT and Ben,

who are wondrous and wonder-full

professors in the School of Parenting,

and with special thanks to all the children

of God from whom I have learned.

Contents

Foreword

The stillness of the winter afternoon was broken only by the rhythmic breathing of my new granddaughter, Elizabeth, as she lay sleeping against my body. Many of the same emotions I had experienced twenty-six years ago when my daughter Emily was a newborn washed over me again. Intense joy, gratitude, and wonder at the promise and potential of a new life brought tears to my eyes. But then I chuckled to myself as I remembered my innocence and ignorance as a new mother. Without extended family close by I relied on the wisdom of "experts." I read and reread volumes on child care and parenting, looking for answers to the questions that raced through my mind. Are the characteristics, talents, and unique quirks of a child's personality the result of nature or nurture? Do our children learn to be like us from living with us, or are they like us from birth? Do they arrive with all of their buttons preset to develop on a timetable as if preordained? Or can we mold, shape, and influence them in those early years to reflect our values and desires for their lives?

When our son, Patrick, was born two "short" years later, I was still reading. How I wish that this wonderful book had been available then. Not only was I hungry for the factual information this book provides, but I needed the spiritual nurturing as well. You will want to read and reread each section as you journey through the wonder of your baby's first year. As a professional educator, I know the importance of these first twelve months. Much of your child's potential for learning is influenced by the sounds, sights, and touch of this critical time period. And your own self-concept as a mother is emerging, too. We are helpless to do it on our own; we need God's wisdom as well as the wisdom of experts. You'll find both in the pages ahead.

Elaine K. McEwan, Ed.D.

Acknowledgments

To Madeleine L'Engle, who first suggested that Shaw Publishers were the kind of folks willing to take a chance on something different;

To David Paplow, M.D., my husband, who is a patient man;

To Cindy Galloway, R.N., the pediatric nurse and friend who makes my office life easier because she cares for our patients so well;

To Joan Guest and Elizabeth Cody Newenhuyse, the editors (midwives?) who have gently guided this book, this baby of mine, into being born;

To the friends and family who supported this endeavor, and me in it;

and to the special friend who encouraged me to paint a picture of what I term "infant theology" and how it ties into our universal human need for spiritual rebirth, I say, "De Colores!" and thank you, kenya na kenya.

At that time Jesus said,

"I thank you, Father, Lord of heaven and earth,

because you have hidden these things

from the wise and the intelligent

and have revealed them to infants."

Matthew 11:2, NR5V

Introduction

What a wondrous gift your baby is!

You know that, of course. Perhaps you're sitting reading this book as you nurse your newborn, or while your infant naps. Perhaps your child is still inside you, moving and kicking, trying to tell you so many things even before birth. Or maybe you are making preparations to welcome your specially chosen child. Whatever your circumstance, you already know what miracles babies are—at least, you know that in your head.

But do you know that in your heart? Do you also know that babies can teach us about God?

The journey through an infant's first year can be a time of tremendous spiritual growth, an occasion for reflection on your beliefs, ideas, and habits. Many new moms and dads find that having a baby helps them—even forces them—to grow up. Many parents report that having children makes them less selfish, more able to focus on someone else's needs. So God can use this period in your life to bring you closer to divine Love and to discover more of the divine nature.

I have dealt with hundreds of new babies and their parents and grandparents. As a mother of two, and as a pediatrician with twenty years' experience, I strongly believe new parents can be refreshed, challenged, and stimulated by opening themselves up to new spiritual perspectives. You can learn more about God, and you can learn more about your baby at the same time.

"How do I do that?" you might protest. "I'm hardly able to find time for a shower right now, let alone reflect on deep spiritual matters!"

How do you do that? You allow your baby to show you.

The development of an infant in the first year of life is, of course, remarkable. She* is changing and growing almost literally before your eyes. And these changes have God's fingerprints all over them. In this book, then, we'll be looking at some of the aspects of your baby's growth on a month-by-month basis, with a chapter for each month. Because I know new parents are pressed for time, I've divided each chapter into a series of short reflections on your infant's physiological development and what that development can teach all of us about God—and about ourselves. (Note: there is a broad range of what is considered "normal" infant development. Your child may fall outside the norm in one or even all of the skill areas described in this book. I have written this volume as a general guide, taking into account an average picture of infant development. If you have questions about your baby's progress, consult your pediatrician or family practitioner.)

And, by keeping a firm mental grasp on what God has to say to you about your child, you may be able to more easily help that child explore her own spiritual journey someday and to develop her own relationship with the Creator who made all things and called them good.

I think that in their infant's first year, parents have a golden opportunity to study Jesus' declaration that "the kingdom of

* Gender pronoun references will alternate by chapter.

heaven belongs to such as these [children]" (Matt. 19:14). One can repeatedly describe childhood using such adjectives as "creative," "open," and "innocent" and still never comprehend the fullness of Jesus' statement. The reader will discover that by living life through an infant's eyes in the first twelve months, one may catch glimpses of the truth of that concept: *child-likeness* = *kingdom of God*. It is not a statement to be analyzed as much as it is a truth to be experienced, a metaphor for the life of the Spirit, a life lived in the knowledge of God's ineffable and never-failing love.

But we get ahead of ourselves. So let us begin.

INTERLUDE

Parish's Four Laws of Pediatrics

I don't have to tell you that new parents are *sooo* eager to do the right thing and *sooo* afraid they'll do the wrong thing. If you're a new mom or dad, you know the feeling! Now that your baby is home and you're well into your new lives together, let me offer some guidance. Over the years in my pediatric practice, I have developed a set of practical guidelines for parents, which I've dubbed "Parish's Four Laws of Pediatrics." These laws are useful for cajoling parents into smiling occasionally, into relaxing frequently, and into understanding that they aren't alone in their struggles. Here, then, are the laws:

1. Parents do better with sleep. I recite these five simple words to each newborn baby I see in the hospital or in the office. While a few parents may feel that this is silly, I believe that infants respond to being spoken to from the moment they're born. I am also checking head control and eye movement as I speak to them (the babies, I mean). I want the newborn to realize that anything he or she can do to let parents get six hours of uninterrupted sleep each night would be a gift not only to the parent but also to the child. Parents are nicer people the next day when they have slept—more relaxed and more apt to be pleasant to the child.

And, by reciting this truth, I am also letting the parents know that they have a right to expect some considerations in life. The give-and-take of the parent-child relationship works both ways. Of course we give to our children; we want to see their physical and emotional needs met whenever possible. But once in awhile it's fair for parents to expect some of the basic requirements for sanity from their kids.

2. All patients get fifty percent better as soon as they reach the doctor's office, or just after the appointment is made. Veteran parents will attest to the truth of this dictum. For example, after a grueling night of sleepless hours because the child is coughing repeatedly, the parent brings in the child to see the physician. Does the child cough even once while in the examining room? Does the car make the funny noise while the mechanic is listening? You know the answer already!

Pediatricians who are worth their stethoscopes will pay close attention to the details parents give about their child's condition. The physician may be called upon to treat the clinical history as much as what he or she actually observes in the office. Unfortunately, most inflammatory processes in the body are more pronounced at night or in the early morning than they are in the middle of the day, so, physiologically, Law #2 makes sense.

Spiritually and emotionally, outside the doctor's office, it makes sense too. Often the simple act of sharing our problem, our "ill," with someone else can shrink the problem and help us begin to heal. This is especially true for new parents, who can think that no other person in the history of the world ever made silly mistakes or felt incompetent.

3. Life's too short not to laugh and have fun. Especially life with kids. A sense of humor and fun is one of the strongest survival skills a mom or dad can master. No, you won't always laugh when you're changing your son's diaper and he . . . lets go. Sure, you'll get exasperated when your baby throws everything off her high-chair tray, and it will weary you to constantly argue with your eighteen-month-old when he arrives at the "No!" stage.

Still, children are funny, and they *love* to make you laugh. If you look for it, you can find humor in most parenting situations. (And in parents, too: we do well to laugh at ourselves from time to time.)

4. Things change. This law is one that offers the brevity necessary for the parent to be able to chant it under the breath in almost any situation, and it is therefore a very pragmatic and useful reminder. If your child is in a developmental stage that's driving you crazy, remember: if you can just wait, it will change.

Prologue:
Waiting and Listening

It's been so long. You're getting tired of waiting, eager to be on the adventure, excited about *seeing* your baby. You think every little muscle twinge or contraction might be the sign of beginning labor. Neither of you is getting much sleep, and the out-of-bed, back-to-bed midnight stumbles to the bathroom don't help the situation. As idyllic as the pictures in *American Baby* magazine might be, the reality at this point is that both of you are suffering from the stress of waiting, and your nerves are on edge. Expectant parents are already learning an important lesson—media images of blooming, blissful new moms and moms-to-be don't have a lot to do with reality. (Have you ever seen a television or film portrayal of a pregnant woman in her thirty-ninth week that looked even *vaguely* realistic?)

But have courage. It won't be long. While you're waiting, ponder this Scripture:

> In those days Mary set out and went with haste to a Judean town in the hill country, where she entered the house of Zechariah and greeted Elizabeth. When Elizabeth heard Mary's greeting, the child leaped in her womb. And Elizabeth was filled with the Holy Spirit and exclaimed with a loud cry, "Blessed are you among women,

and blessed is the fruit of your womb." (Luke 1:39-42, NRSV)

This is a wonderful story of recognition, of reconciliation, of wonder. Mary goes to visit her cousin Elizabeth after it becomes apparent that Mary will be delivering a child under quite unusual circumstances. Will Elizabeth welcome her, or will she reject Mary, supposing that Mary's child is illegitimate and therefore a cause of shame for the family? As we can read in Luke's account, Mary is welcomed not only by Elizabeth but also by Elizabeth's unborn child (John, called "The Baptist") with joy and enthusiasm. And this greeting becomes a source of wonder and rejoicing for both Elizabeth and Mary as they reflect together on the miracle of new life that can communicate even *before* birth.

You've already felt your little one's kicks and turns inside you. You can "answer" him with your voices, with little pats, with music (especially music with lots of rhythm and percussion). Your baby hears these messages from the big world out there, messages that communicate "I love you" to him even before he is born into that big world. Those little rubs you or your husband may be giving your belly right now aren't idle actions; they signal your love and your caring to your baby.

How amazing it is that God creates us with a need to communicate that is so deep and so intense that we can't even wait until we're born! At the same time, our longing to meet our baby is so great that we can't wait either. So we touch and we sing and we speak, and the baby hears and perhaps moves to the beat.

But it's starting to get a little cramped in there. This child, who began as a single cell, has spent the last eight or nine months growing and developing into a marvelous creation of

God, with lungs and bones and fingers, with kidneys and toes and a heart and a brain. He is now ready to meet his parents and see the world—but he does not enter passively into that experience, as we shall see.

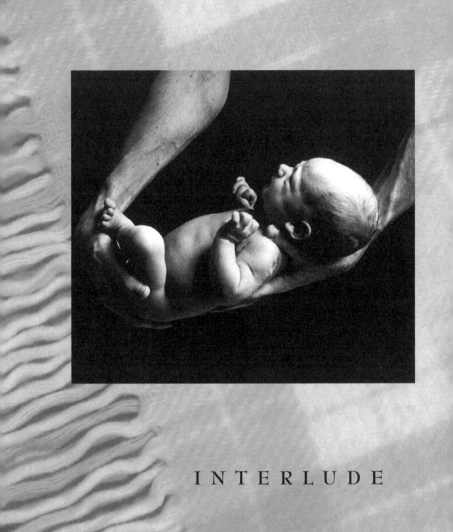

INTERLUDE

Childbirth in Jesus' Day

We are given no specific information about Mary's experience giving birth to Jesus, but we do know a few things about the customs of the era. First, men were most definitely not involved. In fact, after the birth of a child, the mother was unclean for a period of thirty days, after which she cleansed herself with a ritual bath. The "unclean" period of time was longer, and the baths more frequent, if the baby was a girl. This reflects the cultural bias of the Hebrew society of biblical times that males were more valuable and closer to God than females.

Mary would most certainly have been midwifed, probably by the innkeeper's wife or another neighborhood woman who was known to be gifted in these matters. The mother's position for birthing was upright, which allows gravity to work toward the baby's expulsion from the birth canal. We know from Roman records of medicines around the first century A.D. that herbs may have been mixed into an oral potion for the mother. These herbal remedies probably had some analgesic effect, much like salicylic acid (aspirin), and may have been based in an opioid compound, which served as a muscle relaxant for the smooth muscle of the uterine wall. There were undoubtedly ritual prayers said during and after the birth, since the Hebraic tradition was so strongly oral.

"Behold, I Am Doing a New Thing": The Birth

You will never forget the day God introduced you to your baby in the flesh.

If your baby is new, of course, the experience is still vivid in your mind (and likely in your body, as you physically recover from the process). If you're still waiting for your infant to arrive, you're probably feeling a mixture of excitement and dread about The Day. But you won't forget. Everyone who is part of a new-baby experience remembers it as a life-changing event, indelibly etched on the memory.

Every new birth mother can supply a wealth of detail about the birthing experience—just how her water broke, what she felt for the hours before entering the hospital/birthing center or room at home designated for the delivery, how it felt to push the baby out. Or how it felt to have a Caesarean section, how exciting it was to see the baby being handed to her across the surgical drapes. Mothers of more than one child can compare each child's delivery. Mothers who are adopting can recount, second by second, how it was meeting their child for the first time. It is as if our very senses are heightened.

The pain, the push, the joy

What exactly is going on in the mother's body during the birth process?

First, she may experience the sensation of contractions—a cramping feeling in the muscle walls of the uterus. These pains may begin as fairly mild cramps, or, if the mother's water breaks with a dramatic rush, the contractions may begin quickly and build to significant discomfort. Her body is, at this point, receiving the message "fight-or-flight response needed," and an epinephrine (adrenalin) rush bathes her muscles and nerves.

As most mothers know, contractions may continue for minutes, hours, or (in a very few cases) days. These progress to a point of pain such that she needs to use those breathing exercises she learned in her prenatal class, just to get her through each contraction. She's tired, she's perspiring, she may grit her teeth and, with the help of her birthing coach, focus on a particular object. Mothers in the birthing process have been known to say things they later are unaware of, something like talking in one's sleep. (My husband tells me that with both of our children, I announced in the middle of stage II labor that I was going home now, and *he* could have the baby.)

As painful as the contractions may be, they help the cervix to dilate. Once the cervix is fully dilated and ready for the baby to pass through, the mother experiences an intense need to PUSH, to bear down and expel this baby. Usually the doctor or midwife needs to remind the mother *not* to push too hard too quickly, because the baby's head should not "pop out"—this can damage the baby's neck muscles and tear the mother. Again, with the use of the breathing exercises, most mothers can control this almost-irresistible urge to push so that mother and baby do well through the process.

Just after the baby is expelled, a rush of amniotic fluid usually emerges. Then, the baby is THERE, and most mothers are hardly even aware of the passage of the placenta, in their excitement over seeing the baby for the first time.

Fathers, too, experience roller-coaster emotions and often physical fatigue during the birth process. Many new dads cry on first seeing their baby—and, for those few moments, God grants them the grace to weep unashamedly, in sharp contrast to our culture, which discourages men from ever showing such "weak" emotions. Many dads have expressed to me, following the labor and delivery, that they feel guilty for "getting their wives into this predicament," and they may feel helpless over their inability to ease their mates' discomfort. A few brave men have even said they would gladly go through the birthing experience themselves, just to spare their wives the pain.

Fortunately, all feelings of guilt and unease dissolve in those tears of joy when they see their baby "in person"!

It is somewhat curious to me that the Bible does not recount anywhere the entirely human experience of labor and delivery of a baby. Perhaps this has to do with society's traditional reticence about describing such intimate details, or maybe it's because the writers—not the Author but the writers—were men and therefore basically ignorant of the birthing process, since men were not allowed to be present for the event.

Not even the birth of Jesus is recorded in any detail, except to say that he was born, swaddled in cloths as was the custom of the day, and placed in a manger. Perhaps God's Word is trying to tell us that the details of a birth are not truly important. Or perhaps the message is that joy, hope, and love last much longer than the transient pain of a birth experience.

How does it feel to be born?

But what does the baby experience on this day of birth? It is no less a memorable day for the newborn, except that she doesn't really "remember" the experience because the brain is not organized enough at this time to log the information into the central nervous system.

What we do know, from observation, is that the baby tends to get very quiet on the day of birth, with much less movement of arms and legs. As the baby drops down into the mother's pelvic area, the baby senses that she will be needing all the energy she can muster for the events ahead, and she becomes very still.

The actual triggering of labor, those muscular tidal waves of the uterus that dramatically expel the baby and the placenta, remains a mystery. Perinatologists now think that the placenta actually sends out a hormonal signal that announces, "It's time." The child herself is also involved; doctors aren't quite sure how, but the baby may send out a signal to the mother's body ("I want OUT!") or modify the message from the placenta.

Birth is hard on the infant. The baby experiences a squeezing sensation as she moves through the birth canal, which actually reshapes the bones of the skull to accommodate the passage. This accounts for the "conehead" appearance of most newborns who were born vaginally and for the relatively rounded-head appearance of most C-section babies. A baby who bounced on the pelvic bone many times in the birth process will have a bruised appearance to the forehead; the child who descends quickly through the birth canal will have a head or face that looks almost blue from bruising. She may also have petechiae—little red dots on the skin caused by broken capillaries—over her face.

It's not surprising, then, that after all this bouncing and bruising most babies are sleepy and quiet the first twenty-four hours after birth. They appear to be worn out from the ordeal! This may give you the impression that *your* baby will be a great sleeper and give you eight hours of uninterrupted slumber each night right from the beginning. Don't believe it, but do take advantage of that first blissful night to *sleep,* if at all possible.

Think of the changes a baby goes through while passing from the womb to the world. She starts out in a cozily cramped space, with little room to move her arms or legs or head and neck—then she is suddenly pulled out into seemingly endless space, nothing pressing in, unlimited room to fling out her arms. In a matter of minutes she moves from familar darkness to bewildering light, which startles the newborn again and again as she attempts to open her eyes and absorb all the sensory shock of light and shape and movement. (Remember, sight is the one sense she's never used; we think infants have some experience *in utero* with sound, touch, and smell/taste, but nothing can prepare her for the sensory assault of sight.) Up until now she has snuggled in a warm and liquid world, where sounds are muffled—now the sounds are different, louder and sharper and of varying frequencies. Up until now she's felt only wetness against her skin—now strange hands are wrapping her in blankets and diapers and shirts and little hats. And it's COLD!

The newborn has to process all these new things at the same time. And the infant responds to that much change and that much new sensory input in the same way that we adults do—she shuts down for a day or two, becoming quiet, sleeping a great deal, seemingly introspective, as if she's mulling things over. Psychologists have found that adults who are going through drastic change or extreme stress also tend to shut down physically and emotionally, becoming very inward-looking and sleeping a great deal.

Pondering the treasure

All new moms (and dads) know the "ahhh" sense of peace and relief that comes after they gently lay the sleeping baby in her crib and tiptoe away—and she STAYS asleep. There's almost a holy hush that falls over the house; this is the time to "be still and know that I am God" (Ps. 46:10). The infant needs to be still; you, the parent, need to be still.

Just as being born is a stressful event for the baby, giving birth is a stressful event for the mother. Your body and spirit need time to knit themselves together; you need time to process and absorb the meaning of what you've just gone through.

While the Gospel writers don't say much about Jesus' actual birth, it is interesting that Luke speaks of what happened right after Jesus was born and the shepherds came: "Mary treasured up all these things and pondered them in her heart" (2:19). She didn't have a baby book (it's probable she didn't know how to write). She didn't have a videotaped record of her baby shower or a newly decorated nursery ready for the Child. All she had were a few strips of cloth to wrap around her son—a few strips of cloth, and the memory of the look on the shepherds' faces as they knelt before the manger. She "treasured" what they said and, apparently, spent some time quietly reflecting on the great events that had come to pass.

You, too, have been through a great event, an experience that has altered your life forever. It isn't only the fact of a new baby, but everything else has changed too. Maybe you've decided to put your career on hold for a time, and you're wondering how you'll make the transition from briefcases to breastfeeding. You and your husband face the challenges that new parenthood brings to a marriage. All this comes at a time when your physical and emotional reserves are low.

So I would suggest that, during this immediate postpartum period—and indeed, in the weeks and months to come—you allow yourself "pondering time." As you nurse your baby, or while your baby naps, "be still and know" the God who is there loving us, holding out hope for our lives, molding us into beings who can see with our hearts and hear with our spirits. In any birth process, whether it be of the flesh or of the Spirit, God is there to surround us with love.

And, like Mary, treasure your experiences. Perhaps even write down an account of your child's birth to share with her when she is older and able to understand in a more complete way the incredible process by which she came into the world. Remember that this joy is the result of cocreating with God, who is eternal creativity. In the birthing process, you have tasted just a little bit of heaven.

And now . . . you have to learn to live with your little angel!

Chapter 1

Help! We're Parents!
The First Month

The day arrives to go home from the hospital or birthing center. The new parents are focused on the mechanics of getting the baby into his car seat for the ride home, of learning what to pack in the diaper bag, of juggling flowers, balloons, greetings, and gifts. Perhaps they are even trying to impress the nurses with how well they do it all!

The car ride is probably quiet as Dad tries to maneuver the streets with the least possible movement for mother and baby; Mom, ensconced in the back seat, is probably looking at her child to see how he is faring in the car seat.

Then they arrive home, perhaps to be welcomed by a proud grandma or aunt or friend. They wrestle the infant out of the carseat (eventually they will be able to do this blindfolded, one-armed, and in seconds). They go inside and get settled. Look at the baby. Look at each other with dazed expressions that clearly ask, "What the heck do we do NOW?"

The arrival home is indeed an overwhelming moment, and one that often makes parents wonder if *every* moment with their new baby will feel like this. If you've struggled with this, don't worry—you're normal! And perhaps these feelings are heightened by the fact that mothers who deliver normally spend so little time in the hospital these days. To address this problem, the American Academy of Pediatrics is working toward getting legislation passed in all fifty states to keep mothers and babies in the hospital for at least thirty-six hours, so both may be observed a bit longer in case any problems arise.

After such a life-changing experience as birth, it's natural for parents to feel awash in the details of caring for a new baby. The answer I give parents when they ask me, "What do we do now?" is "Live life! You just have a new person in your life to live it with now."

After all, the mechanics of existence go on. The housecleaning, the laundry, the meals, taking out the garbage—all those tasks remain. And, in one sense, all those familiar tasks are a gift because they ground us in the face of this enormous and often-disorienting change in our lives.

It's fair to remember, however, that the new mother has little energy for laundry, meal preparation, or housework. Her job in those first few weeks after the baby is born is—I'll say it again—to REST, to participate in the hands-on care of the baby (who can already distinguish her from everyone else in the world), and to feed the baby. Especially if a mother is breast-feeding, rest is essential to good milk production in the first month of the infant's life.

A word about breast-feeding: some new moms find it isn't always as easy as it looks in the magazines; and, with those shorter hospital stays, there isn't always time for nurses to help mother and baby get used to each other. If you're having problems, I would advise you to consult your pediatrician or obstetrician. Many cities have chapters of La Leche League, and some nurses specialize in lactation consultation. Many hospitals also have lactation consultants who will work with Mom and baby to establish good nursing techniques.

With all this encouragement and expertise on breast-feeding, it's still important to note that not every mother can or wants to nurse her infant. Some mothers get a breast infection, which makes breast-feeding too painful; some are forced to return to work so quickly that nursing is impractical. Yes, breast milk is preferable both nutritionally and immunologically. But if you decide, after trying to nurse for several weeks, that you're going to formula-feed your baby, please don't feel guilty. Do I encourage breast-feeding? Yes. Do I insist on it, or think that your child will be forever inferior if you don't breast-feed? No!

If you're a new mom who's struggling with the feeling that you aren't on top of your household organization during these first couple of months, I would strongly recommend that you try to relax your expectations for yourself. What you are doing is vitally important to your baby's welfare. The housework will still be there when your child is two months old, but what you do for your child right now—the feeding, the rocking, the changing, the holding, the gentle talking—is irreplaceable, cannot be replicated by anyone else, and is crucial to the infant's survival and well-being. Let grand-mas, dads, or friends do the laundry . . . you rest and enjoy your baby!

Will we ever get this right?

Here's something else to keep in mind when the baby cries in the middle of the night and that helpless, *what-now?* feeling assails you again: All of life is "something I don't know how to do" (or, as I phrased it once in a song, "Life is a single take"). You've never lived this day before, nor will you live it again. You and I have faced many situations in the past in which we felt overwhelmed, or a complete novice, or unsure of the next step. That part *is* familiar! Well, parenting is no different. It's a living and dynamic *relationship* you develop with your child over time, much like our relationship with God.

Kids change. Parenting changes. Veterans of the parenting business will tell you that this is only the beginning, that just when you feel you've got this business of parenting down pat, something new comes up! But you will learn. You *will* handle the various challenges that come with the territory; then you will handle them again. Fathers and mothers who worry too much about creating the perfect child or "doing it right" cannot relax and enjoy the wondrous adventure of parenting, and they cannot grow through the process, because where there is challenge, there is growth.

God knows this. Look at the scriptural record. The stories of Abraham and Sarah, Jacob, Joseph, Moses, King David, Jonah, Mary, and Simon Peter—not to mention countless others—show men and women whom God put into situations so they could learn *who they were created to be.*

Through the very process of trial and error, you are learning and growing. It may not seem that way; you may feel as if it's all you can do to get through the day (and night) and hardly enjoy the luxury of introspection. But God is at work in you, and as Scripture promises, God is not finished with us yet (see Phil. 1:6), but will be faithful to complete the work that has begun–in this case, the raising of your child! Remember that the next time you're sitting at home in your old bathrobe, holding your baby and needing to wash your hair. Trust God and love your child, and you'll do just fine.

The newborn's movements: a ballet of life

You'll notice that the newborn infant, in the first days of life outside the womb, stays very curled up in position. He enjoys being "swaddled" with arms and legs pinned tightly to the body, because this is the position the baby remembers from *in utero* (inside the womb). But after the first three or four days of life, the child does not enjoy the swaddling anymore and starts to attempt to move his arms (usually before his legs) away from his body a bit. He may study his hands as they float past his face—only, at this point, he doesn't realize that they *are* his hands. That connection comes later.

The entire first year of life is, in a large-motor-skill sense, a ballet of movement, with motions beginning close to the body and then extending, over time, to command more and more of the space around the baby's body. If one was to videotape an infant's movements in the first three weeks of life, and then slow down the tape a bit, I am sure that the movements would look very much like a dance, a dance that could probably be set to some of the classical works of music composed especially for ballet.

Think of Psalm 30:11-12, with its resounding affirmations: "You have turned my mourning into dancing; you have taken off my sackcloth and clothed me with joy, so that my soul may praise you and not be silent. O Lord my God, I will give thanks to you forever" (NRSV). Surely God has clothed new babies with a dance of joy—shall we join in the dance?

Baby blues

"But I don't feel very joyful," you might counter. "In fact, I'm feeling really down, and I don't know what to do about it."

You may be suffering from postpartum depression. Many mothers experience this to some degree after giving birth; it usually lasts from two to six weeks. The condition is normal, and it is physiologic in nature. I cannot stress this point enough—if a new mother finds herself having "the blues" and is unable to shake them for a few days or weeks, she needs to know that this is her mind and body's response to the rapidly changing hormone levels in her bloodstream. The pituitary/adrenal/ovarian system—really all one "feedback loop"—is regaining its equilibrium after the disruptions of pregnancy. The new mom isn't doing anything wrong, although she may burden herself with that inner message.

Again: you will not always feel this way. For some new mothers and fathers, this is a real lesson in faith all by itself. As parents struggle with those "how-can-we-get-this-right" feelings of inadequacy, postpartum depression torments them with the lie, "You will never be a good parent—you will never be able to do it right—and you will never again get enough sleep to be able to think straight."

It is extremely important for new parents to be patient and know that, as the mother's system rights itself after the major events of the past nine months, she will feel like herself again. If, however, a postpartum depression lasts beyond the immediate six-week period after birth, the mother ought to see her physician to discuss the problem.

Love as action

So why did God plan things this way? Why would a loving Creator arrange life so that humans are forced to make possibly the biggest adjustments of their lives at precisely the time their physical and emotional reserves are at their lowest?

I would not presume to know the whole mind of God on this or any other matter. What I do know, however, is that the thing that keeps new parents going during this time is love—not love as feeling, but love as action. This is the love that gets the dad up at three in the morning to walk a crying baby around, the love that enables the mom to put off eating her dinner while she nurses the child, the love that moves parents to sacrifice their own needs for the sake of their infant. It's the love that vows, "I will not leave you alone." And it's a living metaphor for God's love, which is available to every one of us.

The late Henri Nouwen, in his book *The Return of the Prodigal Son*, makes the point that, as believers mature in the faith, they will aspire to become the parent in Jesus' parable. The same message is given to dads and moms in those first hard days of parenting: as parents act out the love they feel for their babies by doing all the things those children need, so we can see how God acts out divine love for us by providing what we truly need in life. The ultimate act of love and sacrifice was to send Jesus Christ so that we, God's children, might have what we need for eternal life—and Christ, too, came to us as a servant, "emptied himself" (Phil. 2:7, NRSV).

That, in both a literal and figurative sense, is what new parents are doing: emptying themselves, serving their child. What they—what *you*—are doing in this first week is nothing less than acting out a good portion of the gospel. Think about that, and savor those 3 A.M. moments. Your baby is amazing—but so are you!

What the baby hears

A trivia question that occasionally comes up on television quiz shows or popular board games asks, "Which bones in the human body are essentially full-grown at birth?" Give up? The answer is the incus, malleus, and stapes—the three tiny bones of the inner ear.

Every once in awhile I have pondered that fact, wondering what God's intent might have been for that little detail of human design. It came to me one day while I was running: the function of those three bones is to hold the eardrum taut so that sound waves will move the eardrum in certain frequencies, allowing the auditory branch of the eighth cranial nerve to translate those vibrations into sound. If those three bones were smaller in newborn babies than in adults, then newborns would hear frequencies of sound that adults do not, and they would miss frequencies that adults can hear as a matter of course. In other words, they would miss the frequencies of the human voice, whether male or female.

But infants certainly do respond to the human voice, as you yourself may have already noticed. A newborn will probably even turn his head around forty-five to ninety degrees to follow a voice, if the speaker moves.

I often suggest to new parents that they experiment at this stage with different frequencies of sound and note how their baby responds to them. If they have one, I suggest they even try the "dog whistle": adults cannot hear that frequency, and the baby will not be able to, either. Babies love music and spoken words. From the very beginning, they comprehend more than we imagine they do. That's why, from the very moment I meet a newborn patient, I speak directly to the infant and not to the parents. Parents will fill in the answers for the baby, but the child clearly enjoys the interaction with another adult.

If the baby's hearing is remarkable, so is a new mom's (or any mother's, for that matter). I can't prove it clinically, but it does seem as if God somehow ratchets up the new mother's sensitivity to the smallest sound her baby might make. A sleeping mother can be jolted awake by a cough, a cry, a creak of the crib. Mother is wired to hear and respond to her child; the child is wired to hear and respond to his mother and anyone else who happens to come his way; and we're *all* created to hear and respond to God. Jesus often ended his messages with "Let anyone with ears to hear listen!"

We all, of course, have "ears to hear." But are we listening? Have we, like Elijah, attuned our souls to God's "still small voice"? This is something you, the parents, can reflect on even now. Our wonderfully creative God uses a variety of people, experiences, events, and other means to get through to us. While you're listening for your baby, you can prayerfully listen with your soul.

Why is he crying?

One of the most baffling and frustrating questions for many parents at this stage is "Why is he crying?" If you're lucky, your baby is one of those contented darlings who only fusses when his Huggies are wet or he has to wait for lunch. If you're like the rest of us, you find yourself playing a guessing game: Do you want this? No? Then let's try this! Sometimes, despite our best efforts, we never really do find out the reason for the crying, so we rock and sing and snuggle and hope for the best. (And, when all else fails, there's always the last-ditch alternative: drive the baby around town until he dozes off.) But over time, most parents learn to "read" at least some of their baby's cries: he's sleepy, he's hungry, he's bored.

It's important to realize that in the first month, a baby doesn't cry because he's sad—there's apparently no emotional content to crying until two or three months of age. The newborn baby cries because he notices something out of the ordinary, and he's trying to communicate that thought. If a parent was to suddenly walk outside on a beautiful spring day with an infant, the infant might begin to cry, to tell the parent, "I notice that the weather is nice today."

Notice how your baby uses crying right now—it will change over the next two or three months. By then he will have learned that crying is an effective form of communication for getting Mom, Dad, or other available adults to do what he wants—pick him up, move him from one set of arms to the next, walk him around the room. How else is he supposed to tell us?

Of course, when we adults cry, it *is* out of emotion. We're tired or lonely or in physical pain or just plain sad; we're moved or joyful or angry or grief-stricken. Unlike us, God does not have to indulge in guesswork to figure out why we're crying. Our heavenly Parent knows, hears, and answers. And, as new parents find with their babies there are times when only Mom or Dad will do, there are also times in our lives as adults when only God *will* do and only God *can* do.

New moms and dads can feel worn out from the demands of parenthood, but it's easier and more acceptable for mothers to admit their struggles. Dads, however, are usually juggling a job, an increased housework load, and at least some infant care. When all this feels overwhelming, men don't have to feel ashamed to cry out to God. David wasn't; the Psalms are full of such entreaties as "Hear my cry for mercy as I call to you for help, as I lift up my hands toward your Most Holy Place" (Ps. 28:2). David had that sort of intimate, no-holds-barred relationship with the Almighty that God desires with the rest of us. We may, at times, feel like imperfect parents; but God, the perfect Parent, can take care of our needs completely.

Hey, here comes the Old Spice man!

In the first two months of life, an infant's sense of smell is truly wondrous. Babies can identify both Mom and Dad by their odors, so I caution new fathers not to change brands of deodorant or after-shave in this time period, because it may confuse the infant's ability to recognize Dad. We have known for some time that babies can distinguish their mothers from other people, presumably because of the pheromones present in mothers' breast milk. Pheromones are molecules of aroma that seem to interact in some way with the endocrine system, sort of like hormones-in-the-air, not in the bloodstream. We also know that a lactating mother can quiet a crying infant when no one else can. Recently, evidence has emerged to suggest that infants recognize their *own* mother's milk and will consistently prefer that milk out of many different milks offered.

Babies rely heavily on their sense of smell, of course, because their sense of vision is not very acute at this point. Over the next three to four months, the infant "trades in" smell for sight, and by six months of age, we think that a baby's sense of smell is much like that of an adult.

Research indicates that there is a "lock-and-key" mechanism by which a baby recognizes his mother's pheromones—that is, the mother's pheromone molecules act as the key that fits perfectly into the lock of the baby's receptors in the mucosal lining of the infant's nasal passages. Imagine God designing such a perfect connection! Even closer than this connection, Scripture tells us, is the relationship between us and God: "God abides in those who confess that Jesus is the Son of God, and they abide in God" (1 John 4:15). This is a wonderful mystery of intimacy and complete love.

You know those incredible surges of love that can wash over you as you look at and hold your baby. Just imagine that kind of love multiplied to the *n*th power. *That* is how God loves each of us. Not only that, but God *knows* each of us. Once we've opened our souls to our Creator, the key of God's infinite love will fit perfectly into the lock each of us keeps around our heart.

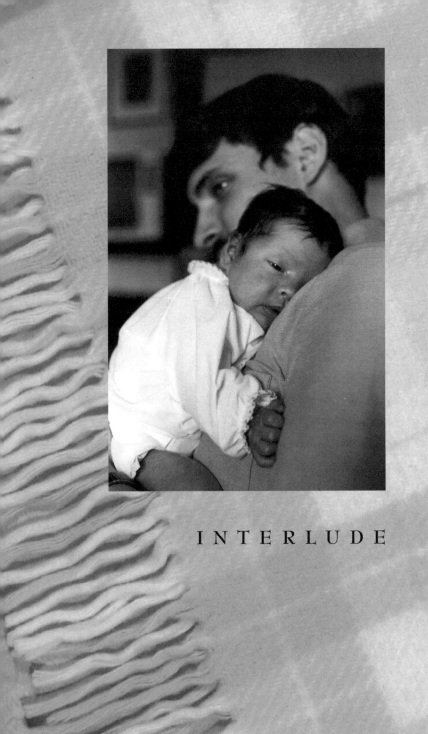

INTERLUDE

On "Spoiling" Infants

It's really not possible to "spoil" an infant in the first four months of life. By "spoiling," most people mean teaching a child that all she has to do is want something, and it becomes hers. Occasionally I'll run into a family where the parents wish to pick up their two- or three-month-old infant to comfort her, and the grandparents object, declaring, "You will spoil this baby!" Then I have to remind grandparents that you can't spoil a newborn or an infant up to about four months of age. By comforting the newborn or infant, a parent is letting the baby know that the world is a place that can meet his needs. Infants who are reared in homes where the basic needs of living are not met grow up to be more suspicious of the world around them, imagining that the world "is out to get them."

At about four months of age, the baby begins to put together rudimentary cause and effect—remember the cough to get an adult's attention? At that point, she will naturally begin a process of exploring the limits of her environment—that's how the baby (or the teenager!) identifies where the limits are. The baby is doing this not to be bad, but as a way of learning about the limits and about what is safe and acceptable within those limits. Limits such as bedtime, when to finish eating (especially solid foods), acceptable behavior while having a diaper changed, what it is okay and not okay to eat—all these things have to be learned, and the teaching begins after about four months of age.

This teaching and setting of limits will continue, of course, until the "infant" turns eighteen or twenty or so. (Society hopes that by that point, the child will be able to monitor her own behavior for the common social good.) I tell parents, "Be clear about limits, be firm about limits, and don't give the baby 'intermittent positive reinforcement'—that is, if she fusses about bedtime, don't go into her room after twenty minutes of crying and take her out of the bed, back into the 'awake' part of the household. That merely teaches her that if she cries long enough, she'll get what she wants! But in the first four months of life, you really cannot spoil a baby—so respond to her cries and give her what she needs, knowing that the time for limit setting will come soon enough."

Chapter 2

Settling In:
The Second Month

As the second month begins, you're probably settling into some kind of routine. You feel more confident about your abilities to care for your child; those feelings of bewilderment have receded as you're learning what to expect and how to cope. Your baby is growing rapidly (just how much, you'll find out at the one-month checkup!), filling out, losing that spindly, thin-skinned newborn fragility. She looks like a baby now. I am full of congratulations for my new parents who bring in their one-month-old for her second weight check and well-child visit. They have lived through this first of many challenges in parenting, and by caring for this small, almost tenuous newborn, they are helping her grow into a real baby. That is a special act of faith all by itself.

I often reflect with them on how it feels to make it through a challenging experience, a time of testing. Mary knew about that. So did Gideon, who clearly doubted his ability to fulfill his role as leader of the Israelite forces and grew through the experience of seeing Jericho tumble to the ground while utilizing only two hundred soldiers. So did Sarah, who so clearly doubted her ability to bear a child in her extreme old age that she actually laughed at the messengers from God—but she conceived Isaac, birthed him, and raised him to adulthood, all while having triple-digit birthdays. Parenting your baby is no less an awesome task, but then, we have an awesome God!

Look, Ma, a hand!

Now, at the beginning of the second month, you can see that your baby is beginning to move her arms and legs with a somewhat purposeful intent. Watch carefully and perhaps you will see your child's arms swinging out away from her midline (an imaginary line drawn down the middle of the body from head to toe), usually symmetrically. You've already realized, no doubt, that your child's wakeful periods are longer now than when she was a newborn and seemed to sleep most of the time. Your baby may spend as long as twenty to thirty minutes of those waking periods studying that fascinating object—her hand! She does not yet know that it's *her* hand, but she's certainly aware of it floating past her field of vision.

At this phase of life, infants pay much more attention to the upper than to the lower extremities, because the baby can see the hands and arms. Her movements are definitely more re-fined, but not yet purposeful. (You may have noticed that on television and in movies, babies who are supposed to be "newborn" age are usually about two months old—you can tell by the head and neck strength and also by the baby's placement of the arms. A newborn, as you remember, will have the arms curled up under the chin, whereas a two-month-old will tend to hold the arms out straight, away from the body a bit. My guess is that they do this because, with a two-month-old, they are more likely to get a shot of the baby *looking* at someone.)

Your baby can now see farther than she could last month—perhaps to a distance of six to eight feet. She is content to sit and watch the world go by for longer and longer periods of time each day. I always counsel new parents to enjoy this stage while it lasts!

Your baby is also watching what you do with your hands. Infants watch and learn from us at a much earlier age than we may imagine.

The hand is truly a complex and remarkable creation. It contains more nerve endings (as we'll discuss later) per square centimeter and more bones in a small compartmentalized space than almost any other area of the body. Its finely tuned actions can accomplish incredible tasks—have you ever seen a diamond cutter at work? Watched Isaac Stern's hands running up and down the fingerboard of a violin? There are surgeons who spend their whole professional career just operating on the hand; it's that complex an entity.

Think of how busy your hands are—gently wiping your infant's skin in the bath, grasping her fingers, snapping up her sleeper suit, lifting her in and out of her car seat. The list goes on and on, all good things you are doing for your little one.

We now know how vital *touch* is in the first months of an infant's life. Even the very premature babies (and I have some former twenty-six-week-gestation infants in my practice, who weighed about a pound at birth) have been shown to do better, eat sooner, thrive more vigorously, when they are touched lovingly. Parents of these babies spend long hours with their hands and arms inside the Isolettes, holding their infants. In situations where parents are not available to perform this caring task, volunteers at the hospital may be called on to touch/hold/talk to these extremely fragile creatures—and these tiniest of babies respond.

Preparing to talk

Your baby is changing, slowly but surely, right before your eyes! When parents bring their infants to me for the one-month checkup, I often tell them, "You'll find throughout the adventure of parenting that changes often happen of which you might not be aware; by living on a daily basis with your child, you are sometimes blinded to small increments of change."

One of these changes which you may or may not have noticed is that your baby is sounding "older," with a deeper cry. The deepening of the newborn's cry happens for a specific reason—the larynx, or voice box, has been very high in the back of the baby's throat up until now. This higher larynx creates a smaller resonance cavity at the back of the throat ("vocal chamber"), causing the voice to be higher in pitch. Also, a listener can usually tell the sound of the newborn cry by the very rapid vibrato (vibrations) of the voice, which can be heard more easily because the larynx is closer to the listener's ear.

What's *really* interesting at this age is that, because the larynx is moving down, the baby will have much greater fine motor control over the muscles and structures of the mouth, called "the articulators," those structures we use to create sounds. In other words, the four- to eight-week-old baby's oral cavity is preparing itself to talk!

Have you ever considered that God may have prepared *you* to talk, to tell your story to attract others—including, perhaps, your baby—to the amazing love of God? True, as the Lord pointed out to Job, no human being will ever have the deep voice of God, nor the awesome power to have created the universe. But we do have a voice, a gift as unique as fingerprints, for purposes of communication with others. How will each of us use that gift?

One of the joys that God has allowed me is to be able to make music, to sing the Ancient Song in some new ways. I have been able to sing, play piano, guitar, percussion, and bass guitar, and compose music since my junior high school days. It is a gift that has been used almost exclusively in service of the church. What a joy to sing and dance with other children of God in Kenya, Zimbabwe, Brazil, South Africa, and even in California! I don't exactly understand what the central nervous system connections are between medicine and music, but I know I'm not the only "musician-physician"—Hector Berlioz and Albert Schweitzer come to mind. (Although I'm hardly in the same league as those two.)

You're using the gift of your voice to communicate with your baby. Sing to her, laugh at (and with) her, tell her what you're doing as you dress or diaper her. Don't be embarrassed to make silly little sounds at her, either! The baby loves this communication and, in certain ways, is learning from it even now. Many months from now, after your child is talking, you may hear an echo of your voice in the rhythm and pitch of her voice. What will she learn to say from listening to your voice? Will she learn to speak the language of love, having heard it all her young life?

The miracle is that God created babies to be so endearing, so winsome, that we can hardly help but speak the language of love to them—with voice *and* face.

God's smile and ours

Surely one of the peak moments of new parenthood is that first time your baby smiles at you! And she IS smiling at you;

it isn't the "gas" of the newborn period. The four- to eight-week-old child is now smiling intentionally at a known person. And that person will smile back, which is critical to the child's social development. We know from studies done in orphanages overseas that children who are not reinforced in that "social smile" will actually lose the interest and ability to smile over time. Fortunately, for most human beings it's IMPOSSIBLE not to smile back at a baby who is grinning ear-to-ear, all for you. Not only that, but at this age infants don't play favorites—they'll smile at anyone, parents, grandparents, siblings, friends, complete strangers in the grocery store! Friend and stranger alike respond instinctively when an infant graces them with a smile, so as a result the baby is receiving much positive reinforcement as she attempts to communicate with the people who come into her world.

You may wonder at this point if your baby knows who you are to her—does she understand that you're "Mom" or "Dad"? Well . . . not yet. She understands that she sees and hears and feels these two large people more than anyone else, but she doesn't yet know that these people are, in fact, her parents. *When will she know?*

You'll find in another two months or so that your baby may realize that a smile may not be enough to get adults to talk to her—that's when infants develop some other "signal" that indicates, "I want you to talk with me now!"

And think about this: we don't reinforce frowning in the same way we do smiling. If your baby fusses at you and looks unhappy, you don't scowl back (unless it's two in the morning, perhaps!). It appears that in all cultures, people smile to indicate happiness, pleasure, or agreement—there may very well be a "smile instinct." In other words, God may have wired our brains for a smile response, and this smile is associated with pleasant things and social interaction. Much like language, it appears to take extraordinary effort to extinguish the habit of smiling in a human infant.

The God who created the universe, and us in that universe, has made us to be social creatures. But beyond our interaction with others, we, the creatures, are made to connect with our Creator. In the Garden, Adam and Eve knew a special intimacy with God, who, even as the man and woman were hiding in shame, walked in the garden and called to them, "Where are you?" (Gen. 3:9). But as a result of the Fall, humanity lost that first intimacy with God.

Yet God still desires to interact with us; and we, in turn, long for glimpses of God's face—God's smile!—in this life. We've seen it in our baby's face, certainly. But we adults, too, can be dim mirror images of God's face here on earth, both to our children and to everyone else God puts into our path. And this isn't some impossible task. Has it occurred to you that even now, at the end of the second month, through your devotion to your baby, you are becoming more unselfish, more patient, tenderer and kinder? More . . . like Christ?

Chapter 3

Born to Hug: The Third Month

By the third month, you and your baby have reached some significant milestones. At last you are out of that difficult immediate postpartum period and are probably feeling physically stronger and more energetic than you did a few weeks ago. This is the time by which many new moms who have been on maternity leave start thinking about returning to work. Some mothers, of course, don't need to work for financial reasons; some do. Still others need to return to work because they would just plain go crazy if they tried to stay home all the time. (I know, because I was one of those!)

In my years of clinical practice, I have witnessed this simple fact over and over again: if the mother is happy, the baby will be happy. If the mother is *not* happy with her life situation, it will be harder for the baby to be happy, to be all he can be. I often have a talk with new mothers at the two-month visit, in which we try to explore her wishes—not what her husband or the checkbook balance tells her is right, not what her mother or her pastor or her neighbors say is right, but what she knows to be right for herself, what God has instilled in *her* heart. And we know that the God of the aardvark and the zebra did not make us all just alike in this way, either—each new mother has to think, pray, meditate, reflect, dream about what's best for her. The "best" mothers are those who feel a sense of balance in their lives.

Important decisions are never made lightly, and there may not be a single right answer for every mother-and-baby pair. Some babies are extremely gregarious and actually do better in the social setting of a caregiver with other children around; some babies are shy and really prefer a quieter home environment. Some moms are lawyers and need to return to their client caseload after a maternity leave; some are teachers and can take a semester or an entire year off. Every mother and every father need to pray about these decisions. Wrestling with such decisions can strengthen our trust in God through all the questions and all the answers. And, whatever the parents' work situation, their baby will continue to be an unending delight.

God's amazing switchboard

Around now you may notice your baby trying to "wave" with the muscles of his upper arm; he may also bat at objects in front of his eyes, especially if they make a noise when struck, like the baby gyms popular now. During the eighth to twelfth week of life, one of the most significant skills an infant is developing is the ability to move his arms in a somewhat purposeful way. The goal, of course, is to be able to eventually move the hands to any point in space, and to be able to put any object—and I do mean *any* object—into the mouth.

The nerve endings mature in a downward direction, from the head to the fingertips or from the head to the toes. Both the connections in the brain (the central nervous system, or CNS) and the connections between brain and muscle (the peripheral nervous system) work better for the upper arm and upper leg at this point in the baby's life—that's why he moves his arms so clumsily right now.

The baby's central nervous system, that "telephone switchboard" of cognition, is very immature, or incomplete, at birth. The brain is present, and the peripheral nerves are apparently in place at the time of birth. But it takes several years for the CNS to mature. The process happens as the number of neuronal (brain cell) connections between discrete areas of the brain increase, and as myelin forms around the nerve. Myelin is a marvelous insulating material that allows conduction to occur more rapidly from brain to peripheral nerve and from neuron to neuron within areas of the brain. You may have heard that infants need more fats in their diets than do adults; a prime reason is to enhance the development of myelin, which is composed of long-chain fatty acids.

Here we see yet another example of God's perfect design. The central nervous system *can't* be fully developed at birth, because then the baby's head would be too big to get through the birth canal. If the human brain were fully developed at birth, no woman alive today would be able to deliver a baby vaginally! This miraculous process of developing new brain power is reflected in the motor skills we see infants gaining in the first year of life; the process continues until the mid-twenties.

The same kind of ongoing development is true of the human "spiritual nervous system." We are born with amazing potential for spiritual growth, for maturity in our walk with God. Often as we grow up in our faith, we leave behind a rigid, black-and-white approach to the great questions of life and embrace a more flexible and nuanced understanding of

God's grace and God's requirements. (James Fowler's book *Stages of Faith: The Psychology of Human Development and the Quest for Meaning* is a helpful and well-regarded resource in the literature of faith development.)

I have often thought that every experience in our lives, and the emotions those experiences evoke in us, serve as the new interconnections for our spiritual nervous system. When we can recognize and live with our emotions, we add to our repertoire of emotional and spiritual connections, which then gives us the insight to deal with new situations in spiritually mature ways. Your baby cannot talk now, but someday he will be able to say "Dada" or "Mama" and know who that means. Someday in the *distant* future, he will be able to say, "Hey, Mom, can I borrow the car?" That's a far more complex sentence, calling on mature (we hope) actions as well as sophisticated concepts.

In the same way, each of us, as believers and spiritual beings made in God's image, grows in our ability to recognize and handle our own emotional responses to situations in daily life. By learning to recognize those emotional responses and to share those emotional responses with God in an honest way (there's prayer again!), we move closer to the heart of God and to the person we were created to be. So recognizing our own emotions, naming and taming them, becomes an avenue by which we gain spiritual maturity. Don't worry—your baby will call forth many emotional responses from you in the next months and years, so you'll have lots of practice at recognizing and dealing with emotions!

The writer of Hebrews seemed to view life in Christ as a process and instructed the readers to "strengthen your feeble arms and weak knees" for the journey (Heb. 12:12). You may feel some days like an object lesson for that verse. But if you look earlier in the chapter, the writer is urging us to fix our eyes on Jesus "so that you will not grow weary and lose heart" (vv. 2-3). Weariness can be the new parent's constant companion. But be encouraged: as your infant is developing physically and mentally, so you, too, are developing spiritually. All these changes in your life are helping forge new connections with God—and you have your baby to thank.

Look, Ma, it's my hand!

The third month of life is a wondrous time for so many reasons! One of them is the fact that the human infant has now truly "discovered" his hands. You might see him gaze at his hands as they fly by his eyes; sometimes infants even look wistful as they gaze at their own hands, as if to say, "Will I ever be able to control these?" In fact, it's probably at the three-month time that a child understands that the hands actually belong to him and might someday be under his control!

Your baby is not only staring at his hands—he's also watching your hands and how you use them. For any activity in which your hands are a distance of two to three feet away, your infant can see your hands moving. Whether you are bathing, diapering, or emphasizing a point of conversation with a friend, your baby is able to see your hands move. Of course, all this visual input probably enhances CNS development, possibly even helping the baby's own hand-eye coordination to develop in a more fine-tuned way. He's learning all the time! Watch how he will turn his hand back and forth (movements called supinating and pronating the hand) to study it from all angles. This exercise is important, because it strengthens those muscle groups that will enable him to grasp objects, including your finger! Many of the muscles that allow us to close our fingers around an object actually have their origin on the bones of the forearm, the radius and the ulna—so coordination of the forearm muscles is important in being able to use the hands in fine-tuned skills.

The baby is now holding his hands straight on the wrists, instead of ninety degrees flexed, as he did as a newborn. This, too, gives those "flexor" muscles much more strength for the action of grasping. Try this: flex your own wrists ninety degrees and try to pick up something. It's harder, isn't it? That's because the muscles are already stretched significantly just from the bend in your wrist, and they don't have much more stretch to give for grasping.

The human hand is a true miracle in its capabilities. I recall that when we dissected a human hand in medical school, I burst into tears just realizing some of the amazing ways that God put humans together. The human hand is not only a delicately constructed and yet amazingly strong tool for mechanical work; it is also a very discriminating sensor of the world around us. Think of the miracle of being able to put your hand into a brown paper bag that contains an unknown object. Usually within a few seconds most humans are able to identify the object just by the sensory input of touch provided by the sensory nerves of the hand! The ability to identify an unseen object by feel, called "stereognosis," is only one of the hand's important tasks—the hand can also give information about consistency of a substance (wet, gooey, hard), size, and temperature of the object and the ambient environment. The human hand can write, play musical instruments, draw or paint, type at great speed, give gestures of affection, and even become a rhythm instrument. It can be an instrument of friendship and hospitality, or it can be used as an instrument of destruction and hostility.

I believe that there are many stories in people's hands. Watch the hands of older people you know, how the hands are muscled, where the prominent veins are—veins grow in size depending on activity of the muscles they serve—and how the hands are used to gesture. I often will comment on the hands of a patient whom I am examining, a waiter or waitress at a restaurant, a perfect stranger—sometimes amazing them if I guess that they might play a musical instrument, do fine woodworking, or paint as a hobby. One can tell many things about people by studying their hands.

And we, too, are written on God's hands, Isaiah assures us. God will never forget us:

> "Can a mother forget her nursing child? Can she feel no love for the child she has borne? But even if that were possible, I would not forget you! See, I have written your name on my hand!" (Isa. 49:15-16, NLT)

Love's most finely skilled creative part supports us throughout our lives. Surely being loved in that care-full way should make a difference in how we live!

Something smells good!

Remember Parish's Fourth Law of Pediatrics? "Things change." Now, an eight- to twelve-week-old baby's sense of smell appears to be changing. We spoke earlier of how newborns identify their parents more by their scent (like Dad's after-shave and Mom's breast milk) than anything else. Now, however, babies with normal vision appear to identify adults less by smell and more by sight. (Sight-impaired infants probably retain that acute sense of smell for a longer period, which would reinforce the idea that the ability to recognize people in the environment is a major purpose of sensory input for babies.)

The sense of smell is governed by special nerve endings in the upper nose, whose path runs straight into the limbic system of the brain. These nerves are slightly different than others because there are no intermediary nerves between the sensory fiber and the brain tissue; what you smell is what you—or your brain—get! In adults, as well, the sense of smell is directly related to the limbic system, that part of the CNS that mediates "intuition" and some of the more abstract memory-linked capabilities of the human brain, as well as some of the pleasurable sensations. You may have had the experience of a certain odor triggering a sudden and strong memory of an event, a place, a person. Some people do have an amazing smell memory. My best friend is one of these people—she's also extremely intuitive, so it makes sense!

It may only be a coincidence (what I term a "holy coincidence"), but this change in smell sensation also occurs at approximately the same time that the human gastrointestinal (GI) tract is ready to handle solid foods. Perhaps this means that the sense of *taste* is also changing to accommodate the variety of flavors we recognize in solid food. We know that adults are capable of identifying many substances just from the sense of smell. Memories of my organic chemistry lab in college return—as we studied chemical compounds called "esters," the lab would smell like bananas, rotten eggs, or a few other choice substances I won't describe here.

Think, though, about how many fragrances you associate with your baby—powder, lotion, freshly laundered sleeper suits, that plasticky diaper smell, the sweet, milky odor of his breath, even the distinct odor of a breast-fed infant's bowel movements. Then there's that indefinable but overwhelmingly wonderful, clean, and innocent infant fragrance. Have you ever considered how we, God's children, may "smell" to our heavenly Parent? It's scriptural: Paul speaks of God's using us to "spread the Good News like a sweet perfume" and continues the metaphor: "Our lives are a fragrance presented by Christ to God" (2 Cor. 2:14-15, NLT). It's amazing to ponder that each of us may be a unique sensory experience for God, which allows God to identify each of us individually. Just as we are written on God's hand, we are somehow engraved on God's senses.

And we, in turn, can permeate the world and change it for good—just as a small amount of a good scent can make a large room more pleasant, so we who name Christ as Lord are called to make our corner of the world more fragrant. And the best place to begin is that sweet-smelling place called the nursery, loving and learning from your baby.

Born to hug

Your baby is trying to hug you. Surprised? It's true: by this age, your baby not only enjoys hugs, he is attempting to hug you back. Granted, these embraces are rudimentary at best (wait until your baby decides to give kisses—be prepared for *wet!*), but they are an honest effort on the part of the child to relay affection to someone else. Sometimes the baby "hugs" by throwing his whole body toward the chest of the person holding him, but sometimes he uses his arms as well. There is a good physiologic reason for this.

Remember that the nervous system matures from the head down. At this stage the baby is beginning to "get the message" as connections are being made between his brain and his extremities. And we know, from dissecting the human body and from a microscopic look at the human skin, that there are many more nerve endings on the ventral ("front" or inner) side of the arms than there are on the dorsal ("back" or outer) side of the arms. Now, just to illustrate the point, assume the position for a hug. Which part of your arms actually feels the body of the person being hugged? The ventral, or front, side, right? So we were literally *created* to give hugs. Hugs feel wonderful to the "huggee" because they are a sign of affection, comfort, approval. But they were also designed to feel great to the hugger—so that, when God is depicted as tending the flock and carrying the lambs (Isa. 40:11), the Shepherd is not only giving, but also receiving, a gift. And when Jesus took the children "into his arms" to bless them, he, too, was giving and receiving at the same time—affection, approval, comfort.

What a wonder that the eight- to twelve-week-old baby is already aware that hugs feel *good* and is willing to interact with another human being in this affectionate way! How often are children taught that human beings outgrow the need for hugs? God apparently never has!

Why do you suppose that many churches are filled with people who would never think to hug someone else in church? It's certainly not biblical to ignore hugs. Perhaps those of us in the church, with the help of our collective infants, can help change the way many people in our own church families think about hugs. They are one of those "one-size-fits-all" kinds of gifts, always renewable, completely devoid of material cost (and that in itself may be an important lesson for our children), and a joy for both hugger and "huggee." How clever of God to have designed us to hug, as well as to be hugged.

One last thought related to the "theology" of hugs: have you hugged your pastor recently? Those good folk need all the approval, encouragement, vision, affection, and comfort—not to mention prayer—that we laypeople can muster. Make a point of delivering a personalized gift to your pastor this week . . . and let any babies in the congregation give one, too! You will all be recipients—but isn't that how the love of God works?

INTERLUDE

On Seeing Colors

Up until now, the infant has seen primarily in black and white, with shades of gray. This is because the retina, the photo-sensitive layer of cells at the back of the eyeball, has been mostly composed of sensors called rods, which distinguish light from dark objects. Now, however, the retina is being "invaded" by new sensors called cones, which make color vision possible. You may notice your baby staring intently at something red or blue for several minutes at a time, as if she's trying to memorize every nuance of the hue. These cones come in two basic variations: red/green, and blue/yellow. The red/green cones appear to "discharge" (fire) when they perceive either red or green; the blue/yellow cones send out an analogous signal to the brain upon perceiving blue or yellow. (This, incidentally, explains some of the phenomenon of color-blindness—the most common variety of colorblindness is the inability to "see" red and green.)

The twelve- to eighteen-week-old infant, now developing millions of cones in the retina, will suddenly perceive the world "in living Technicolor." This explains yet another reason why the baby now wants to be picked up to travel around the room to "see" things—she's trying out her new color vision. Things she has looked at for months suddenly have a whole new dimension, and she wants to *explore* that dimension! Now is the time to replace that black-and-white mobile with a color one. Parents notice that clothing and toys designed for babies this age are very brightly colored now, too—designed to attract the baby (and the baby's parents, who wield the checkbook!).

Color vision is one of God's great gifts to us as human beings. As I sit writing this, I am gazing at the beautiful rhododendrons in my backyard, brightly colored pinks and reds against a bright blue (I term it "uplifting blue") sky and the green foliage of the trees and grass. The wood of my kitchen floor is light brown, with wonderful oak-grain patterns throughout. The cover of my Bible is navy blue. The baseball cap I like to wear while running is denim blue with gold lettering. My son, who keeps interrupting this effort with important—to him!—questions, is wearing an orange T-shirt and gray shorts. My briefcase, which rests on the kitchen table, has a woven, rainbow-colored frontispiece. All around us there is color, just as all around us there is the Spirit of God and the colors of God's love. Do you see them routinely? Do you see them today? Any four-month-old infant does!

Chapter 4

"Look! I Can Stand!" The Fourth Month

Are you still having trouble getting your baby to stop crying? Have you tried walking her around, rocking her, distracting her with every toy in the nursery?

Here's a tip: try standing her up.

Babies at this age LOVE to stand. What's happening is that the maturing of the central nervous system is now reaching the lower extremities, as the peripheral nerves become insulated with myelin. This allows those nerves to speed up their conduction of signals, signals that tell the baby, "Up on those two legs!"

No, of course your baby isn't going to enter the annals of medical marvels and stand by herself. She needs to be held in a standing position, and she needs support under her arms or around her torso to maintain that stance. But she *can* stand, she *loves* to stand, and she *wants* to stand.

Part of this desire, I think, is simply because the child can see more when she is higher. You may have noticed that your infant will fuss until you or someone else picks her up and carries her around the room. (Wouldn't you get bored just lying there looking at the same view all the time?) We all need and enjoy sensory stimulation, but an infant is dependent on an adult to help her find that stimulation. By the same token, a fourth-month infant enjoys standing up because her line of sight is now higher and she therefore can see more of her immediate environment.

Babies seem to be absolutely delighted with themselves when they stand; they uniformly look pleased, as if to say, "I'm so clever! No one ever thought of this before I did it!" It's pretty amusing to watch their pride in their accomplishment. We parents, too, can act as if no infant has ever reached such a pinnacle of ability before—and, of course, the most important baby, *your* baby, never has!

But sometimes we adults can talk as if our struggles, our insights, our experiences are completely unique. And, again, they are unique—to us and to God. The writer of Ecclesiastes, however, notes that "there is nothing new under the sun" (Eccles. 1:9). It's been said that there are only about ten plots in all of the world's great literature (those William Faulkner referred to as coming from "a conflict of the heart"), because these are the scenarios that humans, with a set of predictable emotions and responses, play out again and again. How else could we empathize with the protagonist of a novel, or play, or movie, if we didn't feel a commonality of experience with that person? And isn't it healing to discover that others may have hurt as we're hurting, or may have some of the same problems getting their babies to sleep or trying to balance the demands of family, work, and personal needs?

But whatever our need, God gives us a firm place to stand.

I like to picture myself standing in God's lap sometimes, just as an infant does with an adult. And in the business of standing in God's lap, we understand that God knows each of us individually and makes allowances for our particular abilities to stand.

Picture yourself standing in God's lap today—are you able to stand there, delighting in the moment? Crowing with absolute delight in what you, held up by God's arms, are able to do and who God enables you to be?

Then imagine this: God delighting in you, the way you celebrate your baby, not just for her accomplishments, but because she *is*! That's how God, incarnate in Christ, feels about each of us. So learn to stand in Love!

Into the mouths of babes

Does it seem as if *everything* is going to your baby's mouth now? This period sees great breakthroughs in her ability to explore the world around her—she can now position her hand around an object and grasp the object with a finger-curling motion, to "mouth" the object. Developmental specialists used to think that this was for the purpose of exploring the objects only, but we now suspect that, as the infant repeatedly mouths objects of all shapes, sizes, tastes, and consistencies, she is learning a great deal about the workings of her mouth. As your baby gums your finger, or Dad's necktie, or Grandma's hair, she is actually practicing the fine motor skills used to articulate the sounds of language! She is exploring the use of her lips, tongue, throat, hard and soft palate, and even, in a sense, the teeth she will someday have.

When a baby grasps the TV remote control and slobbers all over it, she is practicing the skills necessary to articulate "yes." When she rubs her face on a soft baby blanket and then mouths a corner of the blanket, she is probably doing a "cross-check" between sensory modalities. When she shoves a golf ball into her mouth and attempts to bite down, she is practicing what to do with her tongue while eating raw broccoli.

All this mouthing activity, in other words, is crucial to your baby's understanding of the world at large. You can (and should!) gently remove undesirable objects from her grasp or put them out of reach, but you cannot eliminate the mouthing behavior—it is too deeply ingrained in the human central nervous system (CNS).

Notice, too, how completely an infant this age is absorbed in the study of some of these objects—she will look at the object, put it in her mouth, take it out again, study its appearance some more, put it back into her mouth. . . . This will occur again and again with the same object. What is the child "practicing" at that moment? We may never be able to sort it out. But the end result of all this practice is a one-year-old child who understands much about the world of basic "chemistry" (what's a solid? a liquid?) and who will have the motor skills of mouth and tongue to be able to articulate "no" and "uh oh" and "aw gone" and perhaps wave "bye-bye."

In watching an infant go through this delightful and moist discovery phase, we are given the gift of watching how intent we could be on living the life of faith—of "practicing the presence" of God, to quote Brother Lawrence. It's easy to put our faith in a Sunday-morning time slot. But just as a baby intently studies an object, so we need to be studying and wrestling with what it means to be the "embodiment of Christ" in the world around us.

Think about how your belief in God may connect to your life on Wednesday evenings at 7:15 . . . to the decisions you are called upon to make on Thursdays at 11 A.M. . . . on Saturday nights at 10:30. Take time to "chew on" Scripture regularly, and learn to articulate those important messages that need to be communicated. Dwell on the joy that comes from tasting God's exquisite presence in all situations. The psalmist reminds us to "taste and see how gracious the Lord is" (Ps. 34:8)—perhaps the four-month-old infant knows more about this kind of grace than many adults!

Voice lessons

You may be hearing your baby a lot more these days. One of the more noticeable (dare I say "intrusive"?) milestones of the twelve- to eighteen-week-old baby is that she is now experimenting with her voice. Just as mouthing objects is a rehearsal for skills she will learn later, these "voice lessons" help her learn the capabilities of this great gift. One minute she will seem to be running scales (making the pitch go up and down), the next she will be whispering, then growling, shrieking (ah, yes), or crowing with delight. The baby needs to learn volume control, pitch control, vocal-quality capabilities, and even needs to experiment with vocalizing while inhaling rather than exhaling.

All of the wonderful things that the human voice can do— listen to Bobby McFerrin's album called *The Voice* for a true celebration of vocal diversity—the fourth-month child has to practice. Every permutation has to be explored and pushed to the limit in order for the baby to find, and know, the voice that is uniquely hers. This should be very flattering to parents, because the baby is working to be able to communicate with them in the future! Finding her voice is only a step along the way in learning to communicate with those in the world who love her, and the baby is motivated to accomplish this step because of a *relationship*.

It is possible to watch a baby crow, and squeal, and growl, and splutter, and to rejoice in the process by which she will learn to communicate with others in years to come. I always advise parents of infants to "Talk to your baby—that way, she will learn to talk to you in the future."

And don't forget that God wants to hear our squeals, our splutters, our growls, and our whispers. God has spoken through all the ages to us, and speaks to us through creation, through Scripture, through the experience of the Cross, and through the events of our lives each day. God is waiting for us to communicate our thoughts and feelings, and waits patiently always.

When is a cough not a cough?

Your baby is no longer a "passive player" around the house! She is getting quite adept at telling you what she wants, or needs—and she doesn't like to wait! What a difference a few weeks makes! Whereas the two-month-old can be placated for a few moments, the four-month-old is pretty insistent that she knows what she wants, and there will be little peace until she gets it!

This is also the stage at which marked differences between individual infants emerge. You may tell a friend about how loudly your infant screams for what she wants, and the friend sweetly replies, "Oh, *my* baby was always so calm." Before you start thinking you're a terrible parent, know that babies handle waiting differently. Some babies are fairly placid, even while waiting—others are SCREAMERS and seem to develop a fury rarely seen within the bounds of the laws of nature. I routinely tell parents, "Whichever your baby seems to be, comfort yourself in knowing that somewhere in the world, there is another infant who is a louder, and quicker, screamer!"

What do you do when you hear your baby make a coughing or choking sound? You turn to your child in alarm or even rush to her side, only to find that there's nothing wrong. What the baby can't tell you is that she's really trying to initiate conversation. This may be in the form of babbling sounds, or it may be in the form of a coughing or choking sound. When your infant seems to be choking, she may actually be doing what we call "one trial learning." She's learned that if she makes a choking or coughing sound, any adult within earshot will look at her right away. That's all it takes! So now she knows she can initiate conversation by coughing, as if to say, "Talk to me—I'm right here! Don't forget that you need to interact with me because I'm in the room, too!"

You will find that this kind of attention, and the success of this signal, causes the baby to crow with delight. She communicated, using her voice! She knew what she wanted (for someone to talk to her); she set about producing the signal (the cough/choke/babble); and the "someone" responded (the desired outcome).

This chain of events is more significant than one might suspect: it calls on memory of an event, a desire to re-create the scenario, and the memory knowledge that the baby can cause the desired scenario to occur, using a vocal signal. That's quite sophisticated stuff for a four-month-old!

Who would ever guess that a baby would use coughing and choking to get our attention? Who would ever guess the myriad and endlessly creative ways God uses to get *our* attention? I'm reminded of that marvelous passage in Alice Walker's novel *The Color Purple*, in which Celie, the main character, and her friend Shug are talking about the nature of God:

> "Listen, God love everything you love—and a mess of stuff you don't. But more than anything else, God love admiration.

"You saying God vain? I ast.

"Naw, she say. Not vain, just wanting to share a good thing. I think it [ticks] God off if you walk by the color purple in a field somewhere and don't notice it.

"What he do when [ticked] off? I ast.

"Oh, he make something else. People think pleasing God is all God care about. But any fool living in the world can see he always trying to please us back.

"Yeah? I say.

"Yeah, she say. He always making little surprises and spring them on us when we least expect.

"You mean he want to be loved, just like the bible say.

"Yes, Celie, she say. Everything want to be loved."

Everything "want to be loved." God wants to be loved and to be heard. So when you see your baby trying to strike up a conversation with you or anyone else in the room, think of God's desire to "share a good thing" with us. Make that *many* good things, from life in Christ to the color purple to an infant who coughs . . . and then smiles as everyone rushes to her side.

INTERLUDE

On Laughter

Two of the greatest moments of my life were when I first heard each of my two children laugh for the first time. As a pediatrician, I was thrilled to realize the CNS mechanisms governing laughter seemed to be functional in both babies. As a parent, I was captivated, enthralled, and grateful to the point of tears. There is no music more beautiful than the laughter of children. At the four-month visit, I tell parents, "Some time in the next few weeks, if it has not occurred already, you will hear your child laugh. Be prepared to be totally unprepared for this event." Laughter in an infant is spontaneous, joyful, unaffected. It reflects true delight in the moment at hand, with no overriding social inhibitions.

One of the most delightful experiences for new parents is to plop their five-month-old in front of a mirror and to watch the reaction of their infant to "the baby in the mirror." Invariably, the child catches the "other baby's" eye, studies the baby for a moment, and then smiles broadly, often bursting into laughter.

What a wonderful representation of the Spirit of God! Babies have no sense of competition ("hey, that guy can sit better than I can!"), no fear ("suppose this kid decides to sock me in the nose?"), they don't worry about being relevant ("so what do *you* think about the paper-vs.-cloth diaper controversy?") or about impressing anyone ("have I shown you how well I can roll in both directions?"). Their first impression is one of delight at the close-up view of this "stranger."

I think that this single-minded gesture of goodwill, with no apparent strings attached and no motive other than hospitality, is a direct reflection of the Creator of all life. Where along the way do too many of us lose this delight in other human beings? How do we become so guarded in our human interactions—in our relationship with God? How often do we delude ourselves that we can hide parts of our lives from God's watchful attention? Do we approach God with a long, solemn face, as if afraid God will recite our litany of human frailties before all else? Do we secretly fear punishment and chastisement from the Almighty? Or can we learn from our children, biological or spiritual, to approach our Creator with an unencumbered spirit of joy and laughter?

When was the last time you imagined God laughing? If it's hard for you to picture, put your infant in front of a mirror right now, and let yourself be reminded of the laughter of Love.

Chapter 5

On a Roll:
The Fifth Month

Get ready. It's time to make sure your floors and rugs are *really* clean, that the dog and cat behave themselves and that no harmful objects are left lying around. Here comes your baby!

No longer is the eighteen- to twenty-two-week-old infant content to just lie on the floor and look around. He wants to get to all the interesting things he sees in his world, to look at them, mouth them, manipulate them, feel their texture and see what wonderful noises they might make. The infant is now, as we say in the business, "a going concern."

Watch your baby, and you might see him doing a sort of pushup. He's beginning to use the muscles of his trunk in the process of learning to roll over. When an infant's torso, head, and neck can form an angle of approximately forty-five to sixty degrees, then he's strong enough to begin the task of learning how to roll over. That's why some "tummy time" is a good idea, even for three-month-olds. As the baby lifts himself into the "pushup" position, using arm and trunk muscles, he will then suddenly buckle the elbow on one side, and *voilà!* he's on his back. This may occur while the parents are watching, but it could also occur in the crib, so if a parent places the infant on his tummy for sleeping, he may roll over onto his back several hours later.

Once the baby is on his back, however, Mom, Dad, or another caregiver may find that he now fusses to be back on his tummy—the reverse of when the baby was two months old! This is because the infant now has a sense of mastery about the environment, and he somehow realizes that he can be a more active player on his tummy than he can on his back. For example, on his tummy he can now reach out and grasp objects that rest on the floor, whereas on his back he isn't at the proper angle to grasp much of anything.

The fact that he may now prefer his tummy is actually what spurs him on to learn the back-to-front roll. This movement calls on strong muscles of the lower back, sides, and abdomen to be successful. The infant will practice this motion with ever-increasing speed, so that by six to seven months, a complete roll from front to back to front will seem to be one movement. Also, it occurs to the more agile folks at about six or seven months that if they combine a front-to-back roll with a back-to-front roll in the same direction, they can actually get wherever they want to in the room, much as a steamroller can roll over the countryside! I advise parents to feel free to hum "As Those Caissons Keep Rolling Along" as they watch this process.

You may have heard children defined as "visual," "auditory," or "kinesthetic" learners. You may get a clue as to which your child will be from watching him roll (or trying to roll!). A visual child may not be very interested in rolling at all—there's too much to look at just by sitting still.

On the other hand, a very intense visual learner will roll with a determined look on his face (not to be missed!) in order to get close enough to study an object. An auditory learner will be interested in rolling to objects that make noise (the stereo system, the TV) or rolling in order to manipulate an object to make noise. The kinesthetic learner will probably be the fastest study on the skill of rolling-as-mode-of-transport—he does it for the pure joy of moving, as well as to see the sights.

It's so much fun to watch your baby at this age, to just sit, enjoying him and encouraging him. It's good for you, and it's good for him. Maybe you've noticed that when you say a few words, he inches closer to you, trying as hard as he can. Then he stops and looks at you; you smile and say, "Come on, you can do it!" and again he scrunches himself forward.

In this way you're motivating your baby, but he's doing all the work. If he succeeds in reaching your chair—or if he only makes it a few feet—you'll scoop him up, hug him and tell him how remarkable he is, and your child will feel himself to be quite the success. And he'll be emboldened to try again (but maybe after a nap).

Imagine for a moment that we, the grownups, are infants on the floor of that room. God is in the chair, encouraging us always to move closer. Do we keep inching forward, looking into our Parent's face for encouragement? If we stumble, do we sit looking bewildered until the Sitter comes and picks us up? Or do we try once, halfheartedly, and wail our discontent?

It is given to some of us to roll, some to crawl, some to walk, and some to run toward the throne of grace—but whichever mode of transport we select, it is our own spiritual journey to move in that fashion toward the author and perfecter of our faith. Babies develop at different stages. So do believers. But God beckons and encourages each of us, every inch of the way.

Hand to mouth

The eighteen- to twenty-two-week-old baby now brings both hands together to the mouth—a skill he demonstrates dozens of times in a day. This is a significant breakthrough, because it means that the central nervous system has matured to the point where motor areas from both sides of the brain are communicating with each other. It heralds the beginning of several developmental tasks that require full-body cooperation and equal functioning of muscles on both sides of the body (pulling to a stand, walking, running, skipping, and much more).

The infant may bring his hands together in front of his face, too. You may find your little darling studying his clasped hands and swinging them gently from side to side. Or he may grasp an object with his two hands coordinated, and then put the object into (where else?) his mouth. The baby still does not use any kind of opposing-thumb grip to hold objects, so it helps to press an object between his hands in order to hold it. This allows him to hold things that are softer in consistency, like food; softer in texture, like a terrycloth stuffed toy; or larger in size, like a ball. The child will also now relate the hands to the rest of his body in new ways—rubbing his eyes when he's sleepy, rubbing his nose when it's stuffy, scratching his head when it itches. (We don't learn to scratch our heads in perplexity until much later in life!)

When discussing this stage of infant growth, developmental specialists will speak of the need for the child to feed himself and the development of new levels of hand-eye coordination. But as you watch an eager fifth-month infant gumming everything he can get his hands on, reflect for a moment on a couple of Scriptures. First, hear the promise of Moses: "There you and your families will feast in the presence of the Lord your God, and you will rejoice in all you have accomplished because the Lord your God has blessed you" (Deut. 12:7, NLT). And then there is the assurance of Jesus: "Just as the living God sent me and I live because of God, so the one who feeds on me will live because of me. This is the bread that came down from heaven. Your forefathers ate manna and died, but he who feeds on this bread will live forever" (John 6:57-58).

It is God's hand that provides the literal, earthly bread that sustains our bodies. It is also God's hand that provides the eternal bread, incarnate in Jesus, who tells us that if we eat of his bread, we shall never hunger again. And the two, the earthly and heavenly bread, come together when we partake of the Lord's Supper.

And it is God's mouth that speaks the Word, which humans, often, carry out with their hands. Hand to mouth, mouth to hand: so God nurtures us and provides for our needs.

Meditate briefly on these questions: how does the hand of God provide for the needs of my mouth right now? How does the mouth of God (the Word) provide tasks for my hands? How can I best be of service in the name of the Word of God just now? And do I have the opportunity to teach an infant to honor the Word of God, and the service of human hands on behalf of the reign of God?

Here's to living hand-to-mouth!

Baby blows a raspberry

It's delightful to watch your child begin to develop language skills, isn't it? Right now, your baby is beginning to mimic vowel sounds. If you sit in front of him so he can watch your mouth as you talk, he will begin to work toward imitating your mouth movements and thereby make vowel sounds.

Most parents instinctively exaggerate their facial movements when talking to their babies—this is probably helpful visual cueing. Imagine the joy, in eighteen months or so, of talking to your little one—and having your little one talk back, of actually carrying on conversations. The fact that any baby is a separate person from the parents, with his own possibly very different personality traits, will be evident when the child can share with the parents his ideas and opinions. Language, of course, is the amazing gift God gave us to be able to communicate with one another; and if you are really interested in a fascinating book on the subject of language and how human beings acquire it, read *The Language Instinct* by Steven Pinker, a neurolinguist from MIT. He makes the study of language acquisition and how the human brain stores, perceives, and deals with language, an exciting story!

At this stage your baby is acquiring language by imitating you. A baby will sit now and stare at your or another adult's mouth, trying to imitate the sounds you make in tone, inflection, actual phonetic sound, duration, and pitch. He's learning by watching and listening—indeed, for the next eighteen months imitation will be his primary mode of learning.

One particularly amusing sound for a baby to copy is the blowing of a "raspberry" (also known as "the Bronx cheer"), where one sticks the tongue out over lower lip and teeth and expels air over the tongue. This creates a wonderful "bubble" kind of sound, usually somewhat damp for the immediate environment. The fifth-month infant, once he has learned to do this, will do this many times a day and then laugh and giggle with delight in his accomplishment. I advise parents not to worry about "social appropriateness": in time, the embarrassing habit will diminish in frequency! But this is a major skill for any baby to develop, involving a deliberate placement of the tongue and a controlled expelling of air to produce a given sound. Wow! That's sophisticated.

While your child is watching your mouth to learn language, he is also listening to the words coming out of your mouth. I usually counsel parents to be aware that their child will imitate, for years to come, the content of their language and the language of other significant adults in the baby's world.

Jesus' words may make some of us squirm: "How can you who are evil say anything good? For out of the overflow of the heart, the mouth speaks. But I tell you that men will have to give account on the day of judgment for every careless word they have spoken. For by your words you will be acquitted, and by your words you will be condemned" (Matt. 12:34, 36-37). If a caregiver is given to the use of "colorful" language, it behooves that person to know that the baby is already imprinting that behavior and that adults are likely to hear that language when the child is five. Think, for example, of how many people use the phrase "oh God" to punctuate conversation—are they really talking to God? Do they really mean to invoke the attention of the Creator at that moment? Or is it just a habit, picked up from parents, friends, or television sitcoms? A baby who hears that frequently in the home will have it incorporated into his vocabulary by age three. Is that "meaningless phrase" (or worse, "using God's name in vain") one that parents really wish their child to be using? It's worth thinking about.

This brings up the entire issue of imitation. We know that babies are always processing more information, and more sophisticated information, than we give them credit for. They do learn to deal with the world by imitating what their parents say and do. I often remind parents, "If you never believed the saying before about 'actions speak louder than words,' you'd better believe it now, because you will be seeing it acted out for the rest of your life! Your child learns best by watching what you do and who you are. Are you comfortable with that kind of close scrutiny? Are you pleased to think that your child will imitate your words and actions? If not, now's the time to get rid of that pesky habit, that 'colorful' language, that addiction to tobacco, whatever it is that you don't want your child to imitate."

Of course, I also remind parents that there are many wonderful things about them that their baby will imitate, too! These are the reasons one's spouse decided to become a spouse, right? I suggest that they keep lots of humor in the home—that's a great mode of interaction for children to imitate. Studies have shown that those who have a functional use of humor can survive stressful situations much more easily than can adults who have no sense of humor. So I suggest, for their child's health, that they remember humor as a survival skill that they would like for their baby to have access to in the future. After all, God has a great sense of humor!

Come here, go away

Babies are the most hospitable people on the face of the earth. They catch the eye of anyone, be it stranger, friend, or family member, and in the fifth month of life they burst into big grins. They are about the business of *looking for* someone to smile at. And they are not picky—watch how your baby will beam at anyone, whether at the grocery store, in church, or in the doctor's waiting room. He now has the visual acuity (fifteen to twenty-five feet) to be able to see people at a longer range; he's aware that if he smiles, others will smile back; and he has absolutely no social inhibitions. Babies aren't burdened with adult (or adolescent) self-consciousness ("what will people think of me if I smile at them?"). They just enjoy people, and they enjoy their own enjoyment of social interaction!

But don't try to pick up a smiling, fifth-month infant—unless you're his mom or dad! Babies at this stage are reticent with strangers; they definitely prefer their own parents and are happy to share that fact with anyone in the vicinity. So at times a baby may appear to be fickle, giving a stranger that "come-hither" smile and then fussing if that same stranger comes *too* close. What *does* the child want?

Actually, this ambivalence is quite an adult response. We can react that way in the big, important events ("I really longed for a baby, but now that transition labor is wracking my body, I'm not sure") and in the small, insignificant situations ("I know we invited the Joneses over, but now that they're going to be here in three hours, I'm sort of regretting it"). Have you ever planned a vacation—then, as the time approached, you began to wish you weren't going? Was there ever a job you really worked hard to land, but then you found yourself dreading the first day of work? Examples of adult ambivalence are legion. The fifth-month baby is only reflecting these same very human emotions. All of us at times are seduced by the desire for new experiences, by the wish for new sensory input. And yet, when we more fully realize all the changes that may go hand in hand with the new experiences, we get squeamish.

The journey of faith is no different. We hear of someone else's "mountaintop experience" and wish we could have a similar encounter with the presence of God. But when we sense God inviting—or, more often, challenging—us to such an encounter, we (at best) hesitate or (at worst) refuse. When Peter, James, and John went up that mountain with Jesus in the experience we call the Transfiguration (Matt. 17:1-13), they were excited. Peter even prided himself on being there ("Lord, it's good for us to be here . . .") and offered to build three monuments—no doubt with a plaque on each that proudly displayed the witnesses' names! A moment later, they heard a voice out of heaven declaring Jesus to be the Son of God; at that point, they were terrified.

This is only one example of faith experiences being both stimulating and terrifying for human beings. Sometimes this "holy ambivalence" allows us to give a gift that we would not have realized in any other way. Recently my singing partner and I have been performing a musical I wrote, entitled *A Most Remarkable Man*, which tells the story of Jesus' life from the viewpoints of eight women who knew him. Just before each worship time when we present this musical, I always feel nervous and have a brief moment of wishing I'd never had the idea to write or perform this piece in the first place. After the service is over, many fellow Christians tell us they've experienced the life of Jesus in a new way because of our presentation, and at that moment I'm happy to have done this work. This is truly a "holy ambivalence" on my part, and I've learned that when I share this ambivalence with fellow believers, they discover that we *all* can give our gifts to the kingdom, even when we're nervous or self-conscious or shy. God will make of those gifts more than we could ever imagine.

If you have the opportunity to observe a five-month infant attracting and repelling strangers, think of the ways in which God teaches us through the use of paradox. The amazing part of grace is that God can take any negative experience ("via negativa") that we might have, and turn it into something good ("via positiva")—a lesson to be learned ("via creativa"), a gift to another, a moment of realization or reflection ("via transformativa")—all of which can draw us closer to the Spirit of Love. Some of the greatest names among theologians have studied the teachings of Jesus from the perspective of paradox, so we will not be about that task here. We will only say that any infant can teach any adult many things about the realm of God and about that adult's own humanity, if the adult is willing to listen.

Chapter 6

Putting Love in the Doing: The Sixth Month

S ix months old—can you believe it? Your baby has now been with you about half a year. It probably seems as if she's been with you always and you can't imagine life without her. At this stage, everything is new and wonderful and fascinating, and you may find yourself looking at the world a little differently because of your baby and her wonderment at and desire to explore everything around her.

And she sure doesn't want to sit still anymore. The twenty-two- to twenty-six-month-old infant is definitely interested in moving across the floor—there are too many objects in the home environment to explore for her to be happy in one place any longer! (As I tell parents at the six-month well-child visit, "No dust bunny is safe at your house anymore!") Infants in the sixth month have varying modes for scooting across the floor—some use the rolling method previously described; some prefer the "military crawl," dragging the body along on the arms; some employ the "rear-end bounce" to get where they are going, bouncing on the tailbone over and over; and some use both arms and legs in an awkward crawling movement. I tell parents not to be concerned—it's way too early for a true arms-and-legs, coordinated "creep" with left arm and right leg advancing, followed by right arm and left leg. That usually happens at eight to ten months. (If any infant is doing a coordinated crawl in the sixth month of life, sign her up for the Olympics right away!)

Often babies this age will get up on their arms and knees, rocking back and forth as though they intend to crawl, but they just can't get started. They appear, and are, full of good intentions. They cannot abide sitting still for more than a few minutes, because the desire to explore is so intense. Once again, their CNS maturation is the step in the process that will dictate how quickly the baby crawls. It's pretty sophisticated stuff to be able to use opposite arm and leg in a coordinated fashion, so as to move forward without falling to the side! I talk to parents about "babyproofing" their dwelling at this time.

Babies learning to crawl appear to be people with a mission, and they are. Their job at this point is to spot an interesting item across the room; to figure out how to get to that object; and to pick up, mouth, and manipulate the object in the process of learning about it. Rudimentary "cause-and-effect" cognitive skills are being learned. The baby is learning something about goal setting and goal accomplishment. Whether the crawling (or the object) is the motive or the method is less important than understanding that the baby is putting together some fairly high-level cognition to be able to accomplish a complex task. Not only that, the infant has been living outside the womb for fewer months than the pregnancy took!

At this point, babies are becoming what I call "self-starters"—that is, parents have much less to do to motivate an infant to learn. Now the baby can motivate herself to learn, just by looking around the environment. Everything is equally fascinating—the brightly colored toy on the floor, the pacifier in the mouth, the container of powder at the changing table, the food in the dog's dish, the stack of old newspapers by the hearth.

Between trying to keep your baby out of the dog's dish and tending to all the other details of life, you may sometimes wonder how you can connect with God outside of Sundays. But there's a lesson for us in the infant's self-motivation and fascination with her environment. We can become self-starters in our own spiritual learning, discovering God in the events and circumstances of our lives and seeking God's face in both the large and small details of our existence. It's easy to let this go and become lazy, to limit our spiritual questions to "When will this sermon be OVER?" and to think that God is to be found somewhere else, not where we are.

But God, of course, knows better and wants to reach us where we are—just *as* we are, making the most of the life God has given us. Babies who grow up in a four-room apartment don't bother griping that they don't have a twenty-four-room mansion to explore—they go about the business of making the most of what they've got! And their learning curve, the skills acquired, and their cognitive and motor abilities are the same as those of the baby who lives in the twenty-four-room mansion.

Is this what Jesus meant when he said "I tell you the truth, anyone who will not receive the kingdom of God like a little child will never enter it" (Mark 10:15)? The infant is driven by curiosity and desire to learn about her surroundings; she's insatiably open to new experiences and information, learning all the time. Do we have that same eagerness to explore the things of God? Have we retained that childlike openness to the adventures God may have in store for us?

As we journey with God, it's important to remember that

just as the baby is motivated by curiosity, so our actions need to be motivated by love. Mother Teresa, whom many consider to be the epitome of selfless service in the name of God, said this: "It's not what you do, it's how much love you put into the doing that's important." If you forget temporarily what it looks like to be putting "love into the doing," watch a sixth-month infant attempting to scooch across the floor—you are seeing determined love at work.

Hand in hand

The infant, now in the sixth month of life, is making new discoveries by the minute! One of the skills that makes this constant exploration possible is the use of the two hands in a more coordinated fashion. Not only is hand-eye coordination increasing, but hand-hand coordination is also being fine-tuned. You'll notice your baby putting her two hands together frequently, often when she isn't even looking at them. This ability tells us several (good) things about the maturing CNS.

The first thing it tells us is that the baby has equal muscle strength between the two extremities. This is good, because the child will be using the hand on either side of the body to stimulate some neural development on the opposite ("contralateral") side of the brain. The way in which nerve signals move from brain to hand is to cross over from *one* side of the brain (where the motor signal that says "move your hand" originates) to actually send the signal out from motor neurons to *both* sides of the body. Every time an infant uses the left hand, that infant is stimulating some new connections between the right and left sides of the brain; similarly, using the right hand causes new connections to develop between the left and right sides of the brain.

Second, when a baby uses both hands, this tells us that the connections from the brain all the way to the motor nerve fibers are intact—in other words, they work! We know that the human brain, when damaged at this young age, has a marvelous capability to heal and to reroute signals around damaged areas of brain tissue. But if an infant is using both hands equally in the next one to two months, parents can rest assured that their child is making healthy connections.

The third thing that normal "two-fisted living" tells us about the infant has to do with a skill we take for granted hundreds of times a day. The baby can now put her hands together, even when she's looking elsewhere. This signals an ability to know where in space our body parts are and, therefore, an ability to better control those body parts. This knowledge is termed "proprioception" (literally, "to receive one's own") and is controlled by the neural connections in the brain stem. The brain stem is buried at the base of the brain; the spinal cord appears to originate there. This part of the brain contains many neural connections that control balance, our ability to move through space, and the proprioception ability.

When you close your eyes and hold both arms out in front of you, you can keep them pretty much level with each other through the use of the proprioception sense. If, while your eyes are closed, someone comes along and pushes one of your arms down by two to three feet, you will be able to raise it up again, still with eyes closed, to almost the same level as the opposite arm, all without looking at your arms. This ability of our bodies to monitor their whereabouts in time and space is both an innate and a practiced skill. When a sixth-month baby is putting her two hands together and looking elsewhere, she is practicing the skill of proprioception.

The expression "the left hand doesn't know what the right

hand is doing" refers to disorganization and lack of communication (and is an apt illustration for the way some church committee structures go about their business!). But in the Sermon on the Mount, Jesus gives the metaphor another meaning. He cautions his listeners: "When you give to the needy, do not let your left hand know what your right hand is doing, so that your giving may be done in secret. Then your Father, who sees what is done in secret, will reward you" (Matt. 6:3). Jesus is speaking of giving and doing good deeds in an anonymous fashion, and he is also alluding to the sense of proprioception. Perhaps this is what the realm of God is all about—so completely rearranging our basic brain structure that we suffuse love into all that we do, all that we think, all that we are.

We know that Jesus was a revolutionary on many fronts— he talked about pitting father against son, mother against daughter, individual against society and the "establishment" of the religious structures of the day. He said that if a person wasn't willing to leave parents, home, family and familiar surroundings, he or she could not be a true follower of Jesus' teachings. Did he really mean to break up the traditional family unit? Was he against allegiance to one's parents? No, he was saying that if a person is truly serious about knowing the God of love in a personal way, then her entire life will be rearranged—even, perhaps, down to the motor-neuron connections in her brain! God wants to be as close to us as our own central nervous system. (For years people thought that the pineal body, one of the structures of the mid-brain, was the "seat of the soul". . . were they so far wrong?)

Watch an infant play with her hands together in this month; marvel at the intricate workings of the brain and nervous system in the human body; give glory to the Creator of this most complex communication network (move over, Microsoft!).

Your own ability to close your eyes and then put your two hands together is truly a miracle—perhaps this is why that posture has become a traditional one for prayer.

Da-da-da!

The sixth-month infant is now delighting in "talking" with adults and will practice far longer than most adults are willing to pursue the issue. An adult can sit a baby in the high-chair and say, "Da-da-da" all day long, and the baby will work to imitate what the adult says. (Do recall that if any given infant is a visual or a kinesthetic learner, she may have a little less patience with practicing consonant use for long periods of time.)

Usually a neutral vowel sound, such as "a" (as in the word "sad") is used to practice the sounds of different consonants over and over. The infant may now utter a string of "da-da-da" or "ba-ba-ba" almost constantly during the activities of the day. But this is merely mimicking what the child has seen around her. When an adult is not talking to the baby or talking on the phone, the baby may have the television or the radio to listen to. The end result is that the majority of any child's day is filled with language, so of course she will develop an interest in replicating this. (The Pinker book *The Language Instinct*, which I mentioned earlier, is an excellent resource if you are interested in the fine points of language acquisition and neural development of children.)

I think that babies are particularly intrigued with language at about this time for several reasons. One of those, as Dr. Pinker points out, is that neural development is probably at a point where the baby can actually begin to mentally process the sounds and function of language. The baby's development is definitely going in the direction of learning-by-imitation, and the child hears language almost all day long, as we said; therefore, it makes sense that baby will be fascinated by language.

Another reason for babies to be fascinated by language is that they watch adults *talk*. Imagine this—you are a six-month-old (or thereabouts), absolutely fascinated by the world of physical objects and your own ability to move at will among those objects. These giant beings who provide food, clothing, and housing for you will sometimes get down on the floor and "go" with you, but they seem to prefer to stand or sit in one place and *talk* to one another! Now if these very large people know more than you do (and they seem to, on many scores), and they think it's more fun to *talk* than to go, there must really be something special about talking. They seem to be able to make each other laugh, which is always fun to see, much more than that "TV thing" makes them laugh.

Not only that—sometimes, they talk to that funny thing called the "telephone," and they seem to laugh and act as if they were *talking* to someone else in the room. Now, if that fairly uninteresting piece of equipment can entice these large people to *talk* and they seem to enjoy the talking, then *talking* must have a lot of mystical significance, as well as being amusing. Besides, it would be fun—not to mention convenient—to be able to say to Mom or Dad, "I'm really hungry now. Could we grab a bite to eat?" or "I have never liked this cat. One of us has to go!" to let your parents know what you're thinking.

As you can see, from the baby's perspective there are many good reasons to push oneself to learn to *talk*. And of course, as baby practices, more and more neural interconnections are happening in the brain. So it appears to be a win-win situation.

Language does not give human beings unlimited powers, however. As much as we could hope for world peace and an end to homelessness, abuse, hunger, and social injustice, the use of language does not appear to have freed us from these problems. We can speak, but others are free to argue with, misinterpret, or ignore what we have to say.

The story of the Tower of Babel has always intrigued me. The arguments over its historical accuracy are less important to me than what it tells us about human beings: we get hung up on language and as a result can't agree on things and can't work together. It seems to me that most of the world's disagreements begin with a misunderstanding of intent, and often that misunderstanding turns on the use of (or failure to use) language.

My singing partner, a speech-language pathologist, and I have found that in our efforts to communicate through the years, often a misunderstanding between us will hinge on the definition of *one word*. Sometimes in a conversation, we have to literally dissect what was said "word by word" to make certain that we know what the other is saying. And this is between two people who care about each other deeply, know each other well, and speak the same language! Think how difficult true communication can be between two groups of people who have a long history of conflict and who speak different languages. (It is entirely possible to translate the sentence "the spirit is willing but the flesh is weak" into "my ghost is trying but my meat is soft"—even synonyms can sometimes get in the way of real communication.)

What a wondrous gift, then, is the knowledge that the heavens speak a universal language, one of praise and glory to God! The psalmist tells us that "the heavens declare the glory of God; the skies proclaim the work of God's hands. Day after day they pour forth speech; night after night they display knowledge. There is no speech or language where their voice is not heard" (Ps. 19:1-3).

When we admire the stars or a rainbow or a blade of grass, we are speaking for that moment the universal language of praise to God, a language not dependent on words. (More like music, really.) We as pilgrims on the journey can know that our best and deepest communication possible with another human being will always be in that "universal language" of praise to God. When we allow ourselves to be vulnerable to one another in sharing what God is doing in our lives, we have opened the channel for communication on that deep, universal-language level. Our deepest relationships in life will of necessity be with those with whom we can share our faith-journey, because these are the relationships in which our communication goes beyond words. The human need for intimacy, I believe, is a longing for someone with whom to speak that universal language—the language of the depths of our souls.

As you listen to your baby going "da-da-da" all day and thereby practicing language, think of that unspoken speech within your soul. How could you, how do you, give it voice in your life? Creative effort is one way. Silent meditation is another. The deep listening to a friend, the listening that hears beyond the words, is yet another. So is the powerful emotive response we can sometimes have when reading a book that touches us to the core of our beings. All these can be avenues to communicating with the Almighty.

Stranger anxiety and leaps of faith

You might be noticing that lately your baby has been having these embarrassing attacks of shyness. She may actively resist being picked up by a "stranger" (the stranger, in this case, being Grandma or your best friend or the sitter she sees every week) and gesture toward the parent, as if to say, "Take me back. Get me away from this strange person!" She may even push people away. Right now, a stranger is anyone the child sees on less than a daily basis, and her aversion to overtures from anyone other than Mom and Dad can be discouraging, especially to grandparents. Believe me, it does get better.

This does not mean that the baby dislikes the rejected person; it only means that the baby wishes to stay with her parent. (Around this age, babies get pretty good at avoiding being examined in the pediatrician's office, too!)

Why is it that infants so actively fight being picked up by "strangers" at this point in life? After all, they crave new sensory input, and a friend, grandparent, or fellow church member can often carry them around to see new territory when a parent is tired or doing something else. I think it is a reflection of their ability to recognize, and celebrate, the relationship with the parent at this time in their lives.

Why now? It has to do with the expansion of the baby's surroundings at this point in her development. Think about this: your baby can now see across a football field, she is developing a daily routine, and she recognizes her home and familiar objects. Mom (and Dad) are the most familiar of those objects; they are the constants that seem to be around no matter what else changes or where the baby goes. I think that the baby is already using Mom or Dad as the touchstone of familiarity in a world of surprises—the "still point in a turning world." Everything else may have changed, but as long as the baby can be held by a parent, then the baby can tolerate the other changes in the surroundings. (Babies are much more likely to be comfortable going to a "stranger" in their own home environments than elsewhere.)

Change is scary for most of us. Remember how we talked in the beginning about those unsettled "what-now" feelings when your baby first came home? And at those points in our lives when we're going through the most upheaval, we feel the greatest need to hang on to those things that are stable and predictable. Imagine, then, how a baby must feel sometimes, and no wonder she needs to cling a little more tightly to Dad or Mom!

Fear of change seems to be one of those universal emotional responses few of us can alter, even when we wish to. Like infants, we all prefer the safe, the familiar, the proven. And there's nothing wrong with that. We need foundations, safe places, physical and emotional "homes" where we're loved and accepted.

But fear of change can also cripple us in our spiritual journeys. Risk and challenge and the upending of familiar patterns are part of how God deals with us. Think about this: if none of us ever took a risk, we wouldn't have married our spouses, we wouldn't have taken the leap into parenthood, we wouldn't have struck out into our careers. If we never took a risk, how would our faith be tested and stretched?

Throughout the Bible, we see story after story of human beings encountering God and having their lives turned upside-down. The three strangers appeared to Abraham and Sarah, and then they had a baby, well past the usual reproductive years. Jeremiah encountered God, and his life was never the same again. Everyone who met Jesus came away different in some way for the experience—sometimes irrevocably transformed, as Saul of Tarsus found out on the Damascus road.

How many rifts within the church have occurred throughout history because someone envisioned change, and that someone was met with the response, "We've always done it this way, and we're not about to change now"? How many good ideas have been lost to the cause of Christ?

So don't worry about your baby's social skills! She's only demonstrating the tensions we all feel when we're confronted with change. She'll continue to grow and progress. And, as you watch her, consider how God is upholding you in Love's everlasting arms, challenging you and helping you take those leaps of faith. As the church universal, let us take a lesson from the six-month-old infant: let us learn to embrace creative, constructive change, honoring those prophets who have the vision to see that "the way it's always been" does not necessarily serve God's reign here on earth. Journeying with Christ calls for risk, but the growth we encounter along the way makes it worth the trip.

Chapter 7

Sitting and Babbling and Other Excitements: The Seventh Month

One of these days you're going to look at your baby—and he'll be sitting up! He's been able to sit with support for a month or two now, and he has delighted in being propped up in the corner of a sofa, a chair, or a human lap. Now, in the next month or two, the infant will suddenly be able to sit, unaided, on the floor. He will probably use what we call the "tripod sit" at first, which involves sitting with both legs out fairly straight from the torso at about ninety-degree angles to each other, with the third "leg" of the tripod being the hands or elbows. As the baby gains strength in the muscles of the lower back, he will be able to sit straighter, allowing his head to be held higher and enabling him to see the sights better!

This ability to sit using the bottom and legs frees the hands to do other tasks, such as manipulating objects, bringing them to the mouth, and so on. For the next couple of months, a child this age will be "fine-tuning" the use of his hands and probably won't make more significant large-motor gains, unless he's a real go-getter! (A few babies will make significant advances in crawling at this time.)

Of course, the ability to get into and out of a sitting position is crucial to the ability to crawl to an object, sit on the floor to look at it and play with it, and then go on to the next fascination. Babies actually are able to maneuver themselves into and out of sitting positions about a month before they sit independently.

The progression of skills in this time period has always interested me. The large motor skills seem "lock-stepped"—in other words, the acquisition of each new one depends greatly on the acquisition of the one before. Sitting, then, prepares the infant for walking, because the muscles of the lower back will not be ready to balance the torso on the pelvis unless the baby has strengthened those muscles through sitting. Once the baby has mastered the skill of getting himself into and out of a sitting position, he's ready to go on crawling expeditions!

In much the same way, we as believers are "lock-stepped" into stages of our spiritual growth. We cannot learn the fine points of service in the name of Christ until we learn to get our own egos out of the way, as Henri Nouwen has observed. We cannot learn to love others in the world around us as we love ourselves until we know what loving ourselves means. And accepting all the parts of ourselves and learning to love ourselves in our human frailty and imperfection calls forth from each of us the humility—that humbleness of spirit—that is of God. If you love yourself, you can forget yourself.

Roberta Bondi, in her excellent book *Memories of God: Theological Reflections on a Life*, reflects that humility is not "about groveling before God or other human beings." For ancient monastic teachers—and for us—humility means "accepting ourselves and others just as we are, limitations, vulnerabilies, and major imperfections included, as already equally valuable and beloved of God without our having to prove our worth by what we accomplish . . . "

The good news is that God wants us to master these spiritual skills, including true humility, so our Sustainer is patient with us, upholding us, helping us to love ourselves as we are loved.

How a baby memorizes the world

We have seen in the past month or so how well a baby manipulates his hands and puts them together. You'll now begin to see, if you haven't already, your baby pick up *two* objects and bring them together in the midline of his body. Once again, this signals a new level of CNS development and sophistication. This skill calls on the proprioception (knowing where the body is in space) we spoke of earlier; it calls on basically equal motor strength for left and right sides; and it calls for a new level of coordination of the two sides of the "motor brain" at one time.

This skill also allows an infant child to "compare and contrast" objects. (Remember all those freshman-year exams in college?) The seventh-month baby now goes about the intentional business of picking up two objects, comparing them for size, color, weight, shape, feel, consistency, taste, smell, sound (when they hit the floor), "throwability," and acceptability to parents! (My guess is that parents react differently when the baby grabs his infant Nerf ball than when he grabs the remote control for the VCR.) A seventh-month baby will sit, happily putting two objects through the paces, and then calmly drop one of them, grab another and eagerly begin the comparison between the objects all over again!

This is specific work for the infant, but work he gladly

does, because it teaches him so much about the environment. He is, in essence, memorizing the world around him, object by object. It is a meticulous task, but the knowledge that he gains now from memorizing objects will serve him well. Later he'll be able to *categorize* objects in many different ways (the red ones, the heavy ones, the ones Mom takes away); then, from that categorization, he'll be able to *generalize* about objects (heavy things are hard to throw; all stuffed animals are soft and fuzzy; Mom doesn't want me to play with any of the sparkly glassware). It's a kind of mental shorthand that allows humans to assess new situations in unfamiliar surroundings and figure out what to do in order to survive in the new situations.

What the baby is really doing is "homeschooling" himself in the ways of this exciting new world. Now, if only we could figure out a way to keep that child interested in that process of self-education, not for twelve years, or sixteen years, but for a lifetime, we would be giving him a great gift. A broad-based education can help lead to understanding—and therefore tolerance—of other places, people, and cultures. It can help teach discernment and foster critical thinking; it awakens curiosity and helps someone make connections between seemingly unrelated situations. And, when we keep learning, life is never dull!

It's the same way in the Christian life. Too many of us stop learning about God about the time we leave Sunday school. Our minds become closed, and we stop making those connections between faith and life. Are we as motivated to stretch our spiritual intellect as a baby is to learn about his world? To read a book from a Christian tradition other than ours, to explore a different version of Scripture than the one we're used to? To go beyond superficiality in our spiritual reflection? God is so great and multifaceted that there's always more truth to explore!

The lively art of "conversation"

You and your baby can carry on regular, inflected conversations now. He loves to babble, and he's learning about "turn taking" in language (that is, you take a turn talking and then you give the other person a turn to talk). These pragmatic issues of language use will serve him well in years to come. The child is also getting faster and faster with his babbling, and this is due to the fact that he now uses repetitive consonants: "da-da-da-da-da-da" or "ma-ma-ma-ma-ma-ma" (to infinity). By not having to worry about changing the sounds of each syllable, he's able to spit out syllables at a great rate. This gives the baby the illusion that he is truly "talking" with an adult.

An observer will hear the infant practicing these sounds over and over as he works on other skill groups (large and small motor skills, to be exact). The variations in tone quality and pitch are fewer now, as the baby begins to find the "fundamental frequency" in his language—the average vocal pitch at which he speaks. By the eighth month it is believed that babies will have learned the linguistic inflection patterns and pitch variations of their particular language. (Language development follows the same course for all tongues.)

The baby is now, literally, finding his voice. He will giggle with glee at being able to "talk" with an adult—how great is the human need to communicate! It's possible to notice, too, that a baby's "talk" is a reflection of those pitches and styles he hears—the baby who frequently hears voices raised in anger will tend to screech in his speech; the child who hears gentle vocal tones will reflect those in his speech.

As we adults watch and listen to an infant during this time of great linguistic excitement, we would do well to realize that each of us, on our own spiritual journey, has the need to find his own "spiritual voice." What are your strengths? What are your particular weaknesses, places where you really need God to shore you up along the way? Sometimes these places turn out to be the most useful for the reign of God. What is your own story, and how do you tell it now? Do you speak best about God to those who already believe or to those who do not yet have a vision of God's working in their lives? The answers to all of these questions will help you find your spiritual voice.

It's time to babyproof!

Around this time I tell parents, "Now is the time for baby-proofing the house, if you have not already done so." The best way to do this is to look at the world from the baby's perspective, getting down on your hands and knees and crawling around each room. Find those lamp cords that could be used to pull down the lamp. Remove those trailing plant tendrils that could go into a curious mouth. Cover electrical outlets with small plastic "plugs"; guard against cuts by locating and removing any sharp or breakable objects, such as pottery planters that could break into shards. Put gates around staircases, and don't forget that a baby can fall from other raised surfaces, such as a hearth, so keep an eye on him. By babyproofing your house, you are actually contributing to your child's social development by allowing him to explore his environment safely, and thereby to continue growing into a social being who is learning many skills all at once.

If you have an older child around preschool age, you may have already experienced her frustration when she's playing with Legos or Tinkertoys, and her baby brother crawls over and wants to "help" with her creations, only to ruin that which she's worked so hard on. Try this: instead of confining the baby, confine the big brother or sister. If you have a playpen, put it up as the older child's "office," where she knows that small objects such as Legos can be played with safely. She can easily get into and out of her office, whereas the baby cannot get in. This solves the problem of much-needed privacy for the older sibling, while allowing baby the freedom to explore the house in more detail.

As a specialist in pediatric emergency care, I make a plea for parents to be very careful with hot liquids. Scald burns are the most common burn injury in infants. The frequent scenario is that a parent has a cup of hot coffee, tea, or soup in hand and holds the infant in the other arm. Baby lunges forward to see something, and parent spills hot liquid over baby and self. Because baby's skin is less thick than adults', he suffers a second-degree burn. I tell parents, "As a general rule, if you hold the baby, don't hold a cup of tea, and vice versa." Of course, dangling electrical cords from frying pans make a good way for baby to pull down a pan of hot grease on himself, too. So do pot handles within the child's reach. In fact, there are so many potential kitchen hazards that when you're cooking it might be a better idea to set your baby safely in his high chair, away from harm's way but close enough so he can see the action.

It might also be helpful for places the baby visits often— Grandma's house, for example—to undergo at least minimal babyproofing, such as a guard gate around steps. It's no fun when Mom and Dad go visiting and have to spend all their time chasing their little one!

Have you ever thought about God's "babyproofing"? In the ultimate, cosmic sense, the Almighty did babyproof the universe for us by sending Christ to save us. Or have you ever considered that there might have been times in your life when your heavenly Parent saw you heading for some danger, physical or spiritual, and rescued you without your even knowing it? Or that God helps the "baby believer" negotiate the snares and pitfalls of her new life?

And isn't it a wondrous thought that God has left us here on planet Earth to be conduits of love and caring for the world around us? When we support a mission project, when we volunteer at the local food bank, when we serve a meal at a homeless shelter, we are being used by God to help "babyproof" the world for others. Just as a four-year-old may be asked to pick up her toys to protect her baby brother, so we are being asked to change the world, to make it a safe and caring place in the name of Christ, reaching out to our brothers and sisters of every nation.

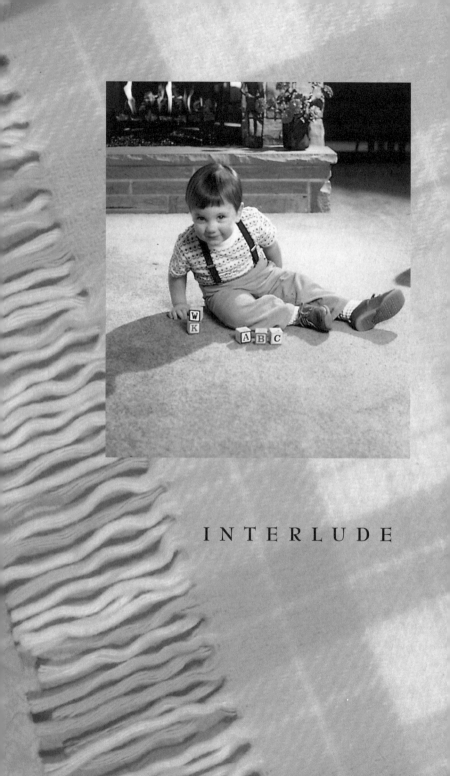

INTERLUDE

What Jesus Said About Children

It's important to note that what Jesus had to say about children is included in all four of the Gospels. Many Bible scholars feel that any topic mentioned in all the Gospels has great significance—so Scripture tells us that children were very important to Jesus!

This is remarkable, given that children were not as valued as individuals in Jesus' day as they are today. Certainly children were loved, just as they are today, but they had no status or stature in society except insofar as they could help with the family work—or, if they were sons, could carry on the patrilineage. All four Evangelists may have remembered Jesus' observations about children simply because they were so surprising!

Jesus spoke kindly of and to children. He often depicted God as a caring, nurturing Father who "gives good gifts" to his children. In several passages, Jesus mentioned that children would "rise against parents" (Mark 13:12), talking about the way in which his views would disrupt the very fabric of Hebrew society. This was a revolutionary idea, for "honor thy father and thy mother" was one of the original Ten Commandments of Moses. Jesus used the example to illustrate how completely the radical love of God will change a person's life—think, too, of how having a child changes one's life!

Everyone is familiar with the story about Jesus and the children who wanted to be with him. The disciples were herding the children away, probably with impatient comments, when Jesus said, "Let the children come to me, for of such is the kingdom of God." The kingdom of God equated with childhood? with birth? Nicodemus puzzled over what that phrase meant, as have theologians through the centuries. And the more they try to analyze it, the more elusive the meaning becomes.

But it's clear that Jesus loved children, cared about them and used them as illustrations of innocence and sinlessness. Some time—maybe while your infant or toddler is napping or off visiting Grandma!—get out your concordance and study what the Bible says about Jesus and children. Then, when you see your own child, love him or her with Christ's love as your example.

Chapter 8

John Wayne Plays Peekaboo: The Eighth Month

Want to see your baby do a John (or Joan) Wayne imitation?

Watch her crawl one of these days. No seven-month-old, as I'm sure you've noticed, is happy to stay in one place for very long. She's getting better and better at "motoring around" the house. She may be scooching on her bottom, or rolling along like the caisson, or in rare instances truly creeping up on her arms and knees. But somewhere along the line, she'll probably try out the "military crawl." That's the one where you scrape your abdomen along the ground as you go and propel yourself using your toes and pulling yourself on your bent elbows. (If you can't picture it, I refer you to any one of a number of John Wayne war movies.)

This crawl is an intermediate step along the way because the baby's arms are stronger and have had more use in the past few months than the legs; so a crawling motion that uses the arms as the primary mode of locomotion would make sense. At the same time, the foot muscles are getting a workout as the baby's toes flex and extend to help propel her body along.

The military crawl is reasonably functional in that it allows the infant to move from one place to another and, assuming that she can get into a sitting position from the crawl, enables the child to manipulate objects with two hands. However, the military crawl lacks not only grace and style (not that any infant cares!), but it is also very slow compared to the true creep. To that end, most babies push themselves to learn the coordinated creeping-crawl; it's a matter of efficiency and speed. Somewhere about now, the infant will grow out of the lackadaisical attitude that says, "there's enough time for everything I want to do," and instead rush headlong from exploration to exploration, as if every second counted in a life-and-death sort of way. Therefore, if there's a quicker way to get from point A to point B, the eighth-month baby will be figuring out how to do it. Be ready!

The military crawl strengthens not only arms but also all the muscles of the "shoulder girdle" (all the muscle groups of the shoulder, a truly amazing joint). This, of course, will serve the infant well in the near future when she decides to try pulling herself up to a standing position. The motion also strengthens the extensor muscles of the leg, from hip all the way to an- kle—which will help when she starts to "cruise the furniture" and take steps along the sofa or coffee table.

The baby puts a lot of effort into the military crawl, but progress can be slow. In the same way, we can feel as if there are periods in our life in Christ that we're trying as hard as we can—and getting nowhere. It can seem that the more "spiritual steam" I generate, the further behind I feel. It's as if I'm getting in my own way (or maybe in God's way) by laboring so hard at what should be a grace-filled, joyous spiritual walk. I worry about my performance, about what people may think, about my ability to handle a situation on my own. But when we rest in Christ's sufficiency, trust in God's timing, and delight in God's gifts, we can stop struggling to get somewhere in our spiritual journey, and growth will come naturally. And, as we grow in grace, we may even learn to walk upright in the faith someday.

Now you see God, now you . . . don't?

No doubt you're playing some form of "peekaboo" with your baby now. Loosely speaking, this is any game in which the child sees something, then does not see that thing, and then can check to see whether the thing is there once again. Dropping bits of food and toys off the high-chair tray, to see how and when they hit the floor, is peekaboo. So is throwing toys out of the crib, to see whether they are visible once they hit the carpet. (Of course, our budding Sir Isaac Newton may also be exploring the idea that things always seem to fall *down*, never up or sideways—and she's testing whether gravity is as effective in the kitchen as it is in the family room!)

Crawling to an open doorway, sitting just on the other side of the doorway, and peering back around the corner to see whether someone is watching—that's peekaboo. So is the ever-popular pull-the-blanket-off-the-head game. All of these amusements are focused toward a single concept: what child-development specialist Jean Piaget labeled "object permanence." One of the properties of an object is that it exists in time and space, independent of the viewer. In other words, "If I see it, it exists—if I don't see it, does it still exist?"

The concept of object permanence is a profound idea, on which much of our understanding of the world hinges. For adults, it means that if your house was on Oak Street yesterday, you are likely to find it on Oak Street again today (for that matter, Oak Street will be where you left it yesterday). This permanence of objects allows us to study the physical world around us and rely on the conclusions we've drawn. It also means that if I put my shoes by the back door yesterday, they will be there this morning when I go to look for them (unless the children have moved them).

For the eighth-month baby, it means that if a parent leaves the room, the parent still exists! At five or six months of age, this same child assumed that parents existed as long as they were in the room and then magically disappeared in some way. Replicas of the parents abounded—a new one existed every time the parent walked into the room where the baby was. Now the infant knows that the parents are permanent. They walk out of the room, they walk back into the room, and they are the same parents as before! This will allow for memory building and relationship building in the future. It's really a very profound thought.

How many adults go through a spiritual quest much like peekaboo? If I don't *see* God, does God still exist? If I have a problem and God rescues me, do I then acknowledge God's presence in the good times? Or is God some kind of celestial jack-in-the-box who pops out to help in the rough times and then disappears again when life is easier? Or what about those times when we're struggling with lack of money, loneliness, fatigue, or some other difficulty, and we pray and pray and don't seem to receive an "answer"? Is God hiding under some heavenly blanket?

Just as we're always there for our babies, whether they see us or not, God is always there for us—one Parent, no replicas. Yes, there will be times when we need to take God's presence on faith, times when we don't feel a warm closeness. But it is that faith that pleases God, who has always existed and will continue to exist and, sometimes, plays peekaboo with us in dramatic and life-changing ways. (After all, consider what your baby has brought you.)

Hey, I'm talking to you!

What a delight-filled stage this is for you and your baby! The eighth-month infant revels in each day, in herself and her accomplishments—and a lot of that delight rubs off on you and the other adults in the baby's life. One of the best, most delightful developments is that your baby is now trying to talk to you!

Right now your child is multilingual, making the consonant sounds of all the language groups in the world: the tonal variations in the Southeast Asian languages, the complex consonant sounds of the Germanic tongues, and even the "clicking" of the Hottentot-Bushman language groups of southern and central Africa. This will change over the next few months as the baby will seem to be a true "sieve," letting in all the inflections and sounds heard in the primary language of that infant's home. By one year of age, the infant will have limited the repertoire of sounds she makes to those that have been reinforced by hearing language around her.

Now it is possible to notice that the baby uses multiple consonants and may also vary her vowel sounds. This certainly tells us that the child has been listening for the past several months! Whereas before an adult might have heard "ba-ba-ba-ba-ba," now the adult may hear "duh-da-ba-ba-buh" or any one of a hundred other combinations of sounds. The end result is a stream of babble that has many of the inflections, rhythm, and a few actual syllables of the native tongue. They just don't fit together in a meaningful pattern yet.

This does not mean that the baby *says,* "ga-ba-dee" but *thinks* she's saying, "It's a great day." She's merely experimenting with sounds and is waiting to see what kinds of responses those elicit. Whether babies think in complete words, or whether they think at a prelingual level, is not completely clear (again, see Pinker's *The Language Instinct* for a more in-depth discussion of this question). The baby is unable to articulate clear words for a number of reasons: preverbal cognition, immaturity of the central nervous system, a clumsy-at-best coordination of the muscle movement of vocal structures, and lack of the crucial concept of words as symbols.

An infant does notice if an adult is listening to her, and she's mightily pleased when she actually gets a listener willing to interact for a few moments!

Our loving God is waiting always to hear who we are, what we think, when and why we wonder about things. God is just waiting to help us learn to sing the song that is uniquely "us" and yet part of the Ancient Song, as well. God is always thrilled when we listen to Love.

The gift of "no"

Up until now, your baby has seldom—if ever—heard a discouraging word. That, however, is about to change.

Your child is beginning to do things you wish to stop her from doing. These include things that might harm the baby, things that require a lot of extra work for the parents, and things that are socially inappropriate. (Although society lets infants get away with running around naked, an adult who tries the same thing gets arrested.) To stop the baby from grabbing the pan of boiling water on the stove is a good thing. So is keeping her from throwing all her finger foods off the high-chair tray and onto the floor (unless you really enjoy cleaning the kitchen floor). So is preventing her from eating the cat's food. It's time to say no.

I find that this is a very big hurdle for parents to surmount. Up until now, they—you—have been the provider of all good things in their child's world. If she needs a drink, they give her a bottle. If she has messy pants, parents clean her up. If she's tired, parents tuck her in. Parents provide comfort, food, nurturance, entertainment, and the community of family and friends. Now, parents must also be the providers of limits. For many parents, this transition is tough, but also necessary. And it's one of the best gifts we can give our children.

Children need to learn early that the world is full of limits. For example, we as a society agree that we will stop at a red traffic light. This is an artificial limit we have imposed on ourselves to prevent traffic accidents. But it serves a good purpose because it keeps us safe. So we adhere to the limit, and we can all (usually) drive safely on the streets. With limits, a child grows into a reasonably productive member of society. Without limits, a child can become an outcast, shunned and even, perhaps, locked away somewhere.

During the next year you will find yourself setting limits and saying no hundreds of times. As important as this is, it does get exhausting. Here's what I recommend: if parents have already said no two hundred times in less than twenty-four hours, I suggest that they scale back to just the safety-issue nos for the rest of the day. In addition, I tell parents to change the environment for both parent and child. Go to the park, the store, the playground, just walk around the block—anything to shift the focus and alter the sensory stimuli for a little bit. Most parents find that it helps both them and their baby. (And, if you find yourself saying no seemingly to excess, you may do well to babyproof even more extensively.)

As you begin the long process of balancing discipline with

acceptance and limits with tolerance, think of how God, in the Bible, balances grace and law, justice and mercy; how God calls for our obedience while loving us all the way to the Cross. God does discipline us; but this, according to Scripture, is a gift: "Blessed is the one whom God corrects, so do not despise the discipline of the Almighty" (Job 5:17). God disciplines us out of love, corrects us out of a desire to bring us closer to the way of Christ. The Almighty is not a capricious, punitive Parent, but One who has our best interests at heart at all times. *Discipline* and *disciple* come from the same root: so following Christ means submitting to, and learning from, God's loving correction. Take some time—preferably after you've finished wiping baby carrots off the floor for the umpteenth time—and ponder this gift.

Exercise: write yourself a letter!

Somewhere between the six- and nine-month well-child check, I suggest to parents that they write a letter to themselves. I say, "Tell yourself all about your infant: how wonderful she is, how much fun she is to be with, a few of the cute things she does. After the letter is written, hide it in your sock drawer (or some other equally secret place) where you can find it again when your child is eighteen months old. At that point, you may need to see in your own handwriting that the baby was a joy to live with, entertaining and amusing and delightful." The toddler months can be stressful and challenging, so the parents in my practice who have actually written this letter have all been very glad, a year later, that they did.

If you are the parent of a six- to nine-month-old infant, go ahead and do it. You may find that the retrospective encouragement gained from such an exercise far outweighs how silly you might feel about writing a letter to yourself now. On the other hand, if you keep a diary or journal, writing thoughts down will feel quite natural. But from now until your child turns, let's say, twenty-five or so, anything you can do for yourself to encourage *you* in your role as parent is all to the good!

Chapter 9

Here I Stand:
The Ninth Month

Your baby is now beginning to lay the groundwork for walking. He's learning how to pull himself up to a standing position. He'll probably try first while you're holding on to him—you may have already found out that he'd rather stand in your lap than sit! One of these mornings, too, you'll go into your baby's room and be completely startled to see that he's pulled himself up and is standing and holding on to the railing of the crib, beaming at his accomplishment.

This is really a complex set of maneuvers when you think about it. The muscles of the upper arm help the elbow move from straight to bent, and the legs have to start out bent at the knees and hips and end up straight, using the large muscle of the thigh, the quadriceps. Also, the muscles that stabilize the hip, the knee, and the ankle come into play, making the entire leg straight and balancing the pelvis on the legs. The lower-back and pelvic muscles are involved too. All this just to stand—something most of us take for granted!

Be prepared for your baby to topple over many times as he develops this skill. He's going to be trying to stand wherever he can—in his high-chair, against an ottoman, grasping a dining-room chair, trying out the tub. All of these lessons need to be learned by the baby—several of them involve bumps, scrapes, and unpleasant surprises. Once again, however, you can be proud of your child's fortitude. As if someone had promised him a million dollars to learn this task, he will go about learning to pull to a stand in many different places, with a single-minded determination that an Olympian-in-training would envy. With this in mind, I suggest to parents that they find two or three stable, safe places around the house where their child could practice this accomplishment.

Images of standing abound in the Bible. Moses stood before the burning bush and was told to remove his shoes, as he was standing on holy ground. The psalmist speaks of standing before God. Jesus was forced to stand before Pilate because standing was the position of respect. Paul reminds the Corinthians, "If you think you are standing firm, be careful that you don't fall!" (1 Cor. 10:12). Jesus is pictured in Revelation as "standing at the door" of our lives and knocking. The heavenly hosts stood before the Lamb and the throne of God in John's vision of Revelation's "new heaven and new earth."

As you watch your baby glory in his ability to stand, think about Paul's admonition to the church at Corinth (which could have been written for an infant, too). Sometimes it's when we think that we're "standing firm" in our spiritual lives, that we're in control and on top of it all, that we get knocked off our feet. But just as the infant cannot stand independently, so we cannot stand without the support of God's strong arm (another image found frequently in Scripture). God wants our complete dependence. And, interestingly, it is when we acknowledge that we are helpless without our Redeemer that we grow and mature in Christ.

Hooray for opposition

You know how your baby has been able to grasp an object (your finger, say) with his fingers since he was about four or five months old? Now he's learning to use his thumb. This means that the baby has a much finer grasp than previously. Try it yourself: pick up a pencil or paper clip using only your fingers, without the thumb. Then try again, with the thumb. See the difference? It's like using a pair of tweezers.

Watch carefully and you might see that, when your baby is using this "pincer grasp," he keeps his index finger straight. There are two reasons for this: one has to do with the build of the index finger, the other, the thumb. The muscles that allow the index finger to oppose the thumb tend to pull the finger straight down, locking the tendon sheath that slides up and down the finger over the first knuckle. In the ninth-month baby's case, he is attempting to move the finger sideways, towards the thumb, as he learns the pincer grasp. This locks that tendon sheath even more firmly, creating the "straight finger" approach. (Notice that when you make a fist, or use the thumb and fingers to curl around a water glass, for instance, it's the thumb that does most of the moving—the fingers pretty much curl in one plane, not moving at all in the side-to-side plane.)

The muscles of the thumb that the infant has first control over are the flexors of the large lump of muscle at the base of the thumb, which also lock the tendon sheath above the joint at the base of the thumb and also over the knuckle. As the child gets older, he will learn to move and control the muscles that carry the thumb into the palm of the hand; but for now, he can flex the thumb muscles and flex the index finger straight down and get the two to meet at the tips!

That's how we humans learn to use our "opposable" thumb.

The opposable thumb, incidentally, is one thing (among many) that sets human beings apart from the great apes such as the chimpanzee and the lowland or mountain gorilla. Their thumbs are rudimentary and set much lower with respect to the palm of the hand, so that bringing the thumb "in" doesn't get the thumb to the palm or to the other fingertips. End result? The thumb in the great apes can be manipulated to hold around an object, but it's not a very fine-tuned process. (Don't look for any gorillas to be playing Beethoven's "Moonlight Sonata" very soon!)

The intense concentration with which the ninth-month baby works at these hand skills is admirable. He will try to pick up everything in this fashion until he figures out that really heavy items are best done with the entire hand, and light, more slippery objects (such as Jell-O) are better dealt with by use of the pincer grasp.

Watching a baby work out the pincer grasp may make you ask yourself, *Isn't it amazing that God allows us to learn new things in our own faith journey and then gives us the freedom to try them out?* It seems to be how humans learn. It's not enough for us to learn a principle—we then have to spend lots of time and energy testing the principle in all kinds of situations, trying and failing and trying again. How patient God is with us as we test the world around us, test each other, and test everything against the truths of the gospel. How many parents would allow their children such far-flung freedom?

How like our creative God, too, to have given us, in the pincer grasp, a visual reminder that *opposition* can be useful! Think about it: we often fail to see opposition as a gift. We wish that our spouse would always see things our way or that everyone on the church committee would come over to our side. Then everything would be settled and easier for all concerned (really, easier for us). But God celebrates diversity. The One who created the aardvark and the zebra and everything in between would of course offer us lessons in the utility of our differences. Whether we are wise enough to see the lessons in "opposition," and to use them for the good of the reign of God, is up to us.

That thing has a name!

Now the ninth-month baby is about to make—or has recently made—a great cognitive leap, a grand "aha!" in human thinking. The infant is now about to grasp the concept that a word is a symbol for something else—an object, an action, an idea. This is a very large and sophisticated leap for the human mind, but necessary to using that most wondrous communication tool, language. Later in toddlerhood comes a seemingly innate sense of syntax and grammar; much later come the pragmatic skills associated with fluid conversational speech.

But for now, the very big achievement has to do with the recognition and acquisition of nouns: when we say "dog" we actually refer to the furry creature who lives under the high-chair and barks occasionally. When we say "TV" we mean the mysterious box in the family room that sometimes talks, sings, and shows pictures even if no one is there to admire them. When we say "door" we mean the opening to the house, through which we go to be "outside." When we say "rain" we mean the water falling from the sky. When we say "baby" we mean the grinning image in the mirror. The baby now is beginning to categorize the basic structure of the language—and it all begins with the understanding that one word is a symbol for one object.

It is interesting to me to realize that babies begin to think about "words" in the same way that older children apparently learn concepts of mathematics; in fact, there are several parallels between the sequence of language acquisition and the sequence of math acquisition. When school-age children are learning mathematics, they begin with concrete objects (nouns) that can be *named* (in language) and *numbered* (in mathematics). Then they incorporate understanding of *processes* (verbs in language, functions in mathematics); and *placement* in time and space (prepositions in language, geometry in math); then they can begin to *modify* the processes (adjectives and adverbs in language, algebra or trigonometry in math); finally, they may use the tool creatively to describe a human or cosmic experience (poetry and story in language, astrophysics in mathematics).

But it all begins with a profound truth: a word equals a thing. Remember the moving scene in *The Miracle Worker,* in which Helen Keller feels the water from the pump and her face lights up with understanding as she finally comprehends what Anne Sullivan has been trying to teach her for months? Things have names! Remember Helen's response? She immediately starts flying about demanding to know the *name* for each thing she can touch. Her thirst for knowledge becomes unquenchable!

If this understanding is fundamental to the acquisition and expression of human knowledge, then how profoundly visionary is the prologue to the Gospel of John, in which Christ is described as the Word: "In the beginning was the Word, and the Word was with God, and the Word was God. He was with God in the beginning" (John 1:1-2). God in Christ rests at the very foundation of human knowledge! Our ability to make any sense at all of the world around us begins with an understanding of, and relationship with, the One who made that world. As believers we are to filter our perceptions of the world through Christ; he is the beginning premise for all we do and think.

Babies appear to be "wired" for words, with instinctive connections and capacities for language use built into the brain. How deeply is God's love "wired in" to our hearts and minds? How can we deepen the connections through which we perceive all of life?

Freeing the angel

This probably won't come as news to you: the ninth-month infant is starting to get into everything. Cupboards, drawers, laundry baskets are fair game. Turn your back and he's after the houseplants, various cleansers, and the family dog. Divert your attention, even for five seconds, and he'll begin eating the newspaper, the garbage, the Phillips screwdriver, or the novel you have been trying in vain to finish for the past two months. The child will cheerfully "help" the parents wrap a birthday gift, or write a note to the grandparents, or even put away the washed and dried dishes—anything to get his hands on something new and interesting.

One of the most valuable disciplinary techniques at this stage is distraction. It won't work forever, but it works right now, so use it and rejoice in the using! "Distraction" just means that if the baby has a Rolex watch in his mouth, the parent needs to take it out and give him something else to mouth (a Casio, perhaps?). If the baby is eating news-print, the parent can take that away and give him the rubber ball he enjoys rolling across the floor. Babies are pretty easily redirected right now. Enjoy it while it lasts! Soon enough he'll turn into a single-minded toddler.

But please, don't yell at your baby, and don't take away the forbidden object without offering a replacement. It's important to keep your voice calm so as to distract your child from the fact that you're distracting him! Besides, he's not being "bad," he's just being . . . normal. You don't want to convey the notion that exploration deserves punishment. And, as we've talked about, babies will mimic what they hear. Screech at your baby, and he'll screech back at you.

Label your baby as "bad," and he will, in time, do his best to live up to the labeling. Please, start now to give your child positive reinforcement. Help him understand that while you may not like what he does, you love *him*, always. Positive encouragement as a parenting habit lays foundations for a lifetime.

The story goes that Michelangelo, the great Renaissance artist and sculptor, found a large block of marble in the junk-pile of the quarry and requested that it be delivered to the studio where he was working. Out of this junk piece of marble came the magnificent sculpture of David, which now resides in Florence, Italy. When asked how he knew that the marble would be a useful piece for sculpting, Michelangelo replied, "I saw an angel in that piece of marble, and I had to free it." That's how we should be for our children: we should always be able to see the angel inside and work to free it. There will be many days along the way when parents are convinced (and in human terms, they are right!) that only God perceives the angel in their offspring—but that is the parent's calling, as the mother or father of this marvelous creation who is a child of God. And I believe the Michelangelo story (whether fact or legend) epitomizes how God sees each one of us—Love sees the angel inside each of us, which longs to be freed. If we let

God's Spirit, exemplified in Christ, work in our lives, that angel can come fluttering out.

When you look at a ninth-month baby, do you see the angel waiting to be freed? Do you see the angel when you look in the mirror? God does!

Chapter 10

Let's Go Cruising!
The Tenth Month

L ast month your baby, more than likely, pulled herself into a standing position, and you marveled at her accomplishment. Well—it's time for the next big steps (literally). Now not only will she stand, she'll begin to take some steps while hanging on to large and stable objects, usually chairs, tables, couches, and so on. In pediatric parlance this is called "cruising the furniture." What it means is that the baby is close to walking!

Cruising the furniture is more intricate than pulling to a stand, obviously. It requires that the child be able to pull to a stand; but then she has to be able to balance the upper body on the pelvis while moving the legs under the pelvis—tricky stuff for someone who can't yet say her name! It calls on muscle strength from the head and neck (supporting the head on the torso), from the shoulder and elbow (for upper-body support), from the back muscles and abdominal muscles (balancing the torso), from the pelvic and hip muscles (stabilizing and balancing everything on this base called the pelvis), from the thighs (locking of the knees and ankles), and from the calf muscles (for purposes of picking up the foot to plant it for the next step).

Meanwhile, the brain stem is keeping the body aware of its

whereabouts in time and space, so that the baby can practice these movements more quickly with each trial run. All of this muscle activity, of course, has to be synchronously timed using the brain's interconnecting capabilities. This is truly a feat of complexity rivaling a NASA space launch—and babies not only do this at eight to ten months of age, they laugh as they accomplish it!

By now you can start to see how the large-motor development has been carefully designed to work one muscle group and then the next, so that the baby is ready to pursue the next step of skill development in a logical fashion. God has designed our own spiritual walks with a progression of development every bit as logical as the baby's ability to cruise the furniture. If we are "babes in Christ," we aren't expected to have the wisdom that a mature veteran in the faith has reaped over the years. If, on the other hand, we're the seasoned "spiritual adult," God expects us to gently bring along those who are still taking baby steps—remember how Paul admonishes the Corinthians against causing the "weaker brother" to stumble. And any of us, no matter what our spiritual maturity, will stumble sometimes! Ultimately we are all called to love one another as Christ loved us (see 1 John) and to nurture one another in the faith. As you watch a tenth-month infant cruise the furniture, remember that we who are the church are called not to count how often each of us might fall but to cheer each other on as we negotiate the pitfalls of this life, and so help to build a true community in Christ here on earth.

Holding toys and bearing burdens

Where did your quiet, contented baby go?

Remember several months back I counseled you to enjoy that period, those weeks when your infant sat quietly in her special seat on the kitchen table and looked happily around the room, hardly making a sound? That same baby now appears to have limitless energy, energy she uses to wreak havoc at a great rate around the house. She now motors around the house with loud squeals, growls, and cries, and she moves almost as fast as parents can (perhaps faster, if it's been a bad day at the office). One of the infant's great joys now is to be able to hold an object most of the time as she scoots around the home environment.

As we've talked about, the baby enjoys holding an object for purposes of exploring every conceivable facet of the thing. In fact, she now enjoys holding on to two objects and comparing and contrasting those two most of the time. This helps her learn about the environment, about size and shape and color and weight. It also now serves the purpose of occupying her hands, so that the infant is learning to balance better over time *without the use of her hands*.

Think how significant this is! After all, we don't use our hands when we walk, and in a month or two, the child will be doing just that. Can you imagine being forced to choose: do I walk or do I carry something with my hands? When your baby crawls around the house holding her favorite toy, she isn't just playing. She's doing important developmental work.

I find it interesting to realize that the progression of skills here is not "walk and then carry," it is really "carry and then walk." Is this a metaphor for our Christian life in community? Are we called to carry another's burden, or even physically carry a fellow pilgrim, at times when we do not feel equipped to "walk" ourselves? Since the carrying comes first, is it not a more profound Christian characteristic than the ability to stride around the face of the earth? Carrying someone else's burden is an act of unselfish love, of service—much as Jesus took on the form of a servant. It is even more sacrificial when we, the burden-bearers, are ourselves needy and struggling. Maybe we need to forget about being prepared or equipped to serve others and simply launch ourselves, warts and all, into the fray of a hurting world—ready or not!

Baby speaks, God listens

The tenth-month infant is now chattering a blue streak. She very much enjoys any kind of interaction with adults, and talking is no exception. It is as important for parents to talk with their infants right now as it is for them to communicate with each other, friends, and church family. Your baby is counting on you (and other adults) to converse with her.

Remember how we said that the baby learns turn taking in conversation from having "conversations" with adults. Granted, the conversational content will be largely a mystery to you— but you've been willing to roll a ball to the baby when you could actually throw it much farther, and you've been willing to "dance" with the baby to music when it would have been much easier to dance without the infant in your arms. So now it's time to talk!

The tenth-month infant learns more than turn taking from these conversations; she learns that she is important to the parents in a social sense. She sees parents routinely turn their "conversational eye" on many other people, some of whom they know and some of whom they do not know. The message from the parent—"You're important enough to talk to"—is a vital one for the infant's self-esteem.

She is also learning inflection usage. A conversation is often a series of questions, followed by answers from the other party. The inflection used in the parents' own language to ask questions is a learned phenomenon for any child. So the baby learns that if one asks a question, one raises the vocal pitch in a certain way, and then the answer usually includes a different vocal pitch from the respondent. These are important social skills to acquire, and they give the infant confidence that language is, in fact, attainable.

Babies need to know, too, that language can be a pleasant thing. Right about now, parents are probably having to say no to their babies many times in a day, while removing from baby's hands items that the parents wish to preserve intact. Having "conversations" with the baby reminds both parent and infant that language is more than a large person repeatedly barking "No!" and that more pleasant times of dialogue are ahead.

Finally, having "conversations" with the baby says clearly to the child, "I respect who you are, I will learn to value your opinions, and I believe that what you have to offer is important." This is an important reminder for both parent and infant that their relationship is a two-way street.

So, for what it teaches the baby about the "pragmatics" of language use and for the unspoken messages it gives the infant about her worth, I tell parents, "Talk to your baby! Now is a great time to get in the habit of having conversation *not* charged with emotional content. There will be time for highly charged talk later!"

Have you ever wondered how it is that God could "think small enough" to converse with us? Here we are, mortal creatures who live for maybe seventy or eighty years, just long enough to begin to have a little wisdom about existence, and then we die. Many of us never think through the deeper questions of life and meaning and purpose. We live in a world whose priorities are all askew, a world whose environment has been despoiled mostly because of us, the people who were supposed to steward creation. We live in a world where cruelty and injustice and—maybe the worst—apathy are the rule, and kindness and fairness and caring the exception.

And through all of that—despite all that—God is speaking to us.

God, who set the galaxies in motion. God, who in a "moment"—however long that may be in divine time, or *kairos*—created thistles and sea lions and lobsters and ladybugs and even, with a touch of humor, cobbled together the giraffe. God, who organized every one of the ten million neurons in your brain and also organized all the neurons in the brains of the other five billion people on this planet. This God, so complex we cannot even begin to think about the divine nature, is waiting to talk to each of us on a personal, intimate level. How do you suppose God can become so small as to think enough like we do to even attempt communication?

Yes, God became man in the person of Jesus Christ. But still, it's a mystery and a wonder how God could become small and finite, fully human and fully divine. There, too, is a mystery! I guess I'll have to add the question to the list of 386,000 or so questions I want to ask in heaven. The really good news is that there will be "time" there for all of my questions and that the God of whom I desire to ask the questions will be waiting to talk with me—then, as now.

God's mimics

You've realized that your baby's trying to talk—in fact, you could hardly miss it! But are you also aware that she's attempting to use gestures to punctuate conversation? She sees the world around her gesture with speech. You may "talk with your hands," your pastor or priest preaches with the use of gestures, even the weather forecaster on the TV news gestures and points at maps and illustrations as he or she talks about the "cold front emerging." A tenth-month infant, being the excellent mimic that all infants are, takes all that in and tries to copy the motions.

This skill actually combines the language/communication group of skills with the social skills, and it reflects how quickly the infant's brain is working within the context of language. In order to point at someone or something on a certain word in the sentence, one's CNS has to be quite fine-tuned and quick, to keep up with the rapidity of speech. To change the gesture once per sentence requires even more speed—to perform several gestures in a single phrase requires precision and speed previously unknown and untried in the baby's repertoire of skills. But an observer can watch the infant practice this many times a day.

The gestures usually are quite rudimentary: the infant may raise her arms or slap her hand on the table with each syllable. (Move over, Khrushchev!) She may point at something definite, but it's more likely to be a simple jabbing motion in the air. She may also nod her head yes or shake it no, or you might see her shrug her shoulders or make a sort of twisting motion of the shoulders and arms. Perhaps if more of us did aerobics as we spoke, we'd be in better physical shape as a nation! All of these gestures, and dozens more, may be employed by the infant to drive home her point.

And by now, you may be starting to see yourself in your baby, and it may feel uncomfortable at times as you catch a gesture or tone or mood or action and realize, *Wait a minute—*

that's what I *do!* Babies truly show us the best and worst we can be.

Babies are natural imitators of their parents. Is this what Jesus meant when he said, "Unless you change and become like little children, you will never enter the kingdom of heaven" (Matt. 18:3)? God has instilled in each of us a longing for communion with our Creator. Shouldn't it be natural, then, to imitate the goodness, kindness, patience, faithfulness, joy, love, and peace of God? At times when you are able to display those characteristics in your own life, haven't you felt a deep sense of peace and balance?

As you watch a tenth-month infant gesture furiously while babbling away, ask yourself in what ways you are learning to be God's mimic.

Chapter 11

Feasts and Faces and Fun: The Eleventh Month

Have you tried "walking" your baby around the room yet, holding his hands and letting him see the sights? If not, try it today—he'll love it. This activity allows him to ambulate to places where there's no furniture to hang on to, and explore further than before, and especially to see faces! When you think about it, cruising the furniture has its limitations; most furniture is against a wall and the baby has to keep his back turned and miss out on the action. Not much fun!

But when the infant has the freedom to move about the middle of the room-space, he can look at people, even if they are across the room, and make eye and smile contact. And this performance generally wins him attention and applause—"Good job there, guy!" or "My, aren't you big stuff!" This positive encouragement is something that the infant unabashedly loves, and cultivates—no guilt, no "aw, gosh, anybody could have done it"—all babies *love* to be praised. Of course the child prefers to walk with a parent across the middle of the room!

Parents would like to think that the most important reason the baby loves to walk with them is for their companionship or for the extra support. But the infant isn't really aware of the support being given by the parent—he just accepts it as coming from "somewhere" and uses it to ambulate. He's also more aware of the other faces across the room, which he can see "right side up," than he is of Mom or Dad. But don't worry, parents—your baby is learning a great deal from this activity. He's getting more practice in balancing his torso on his pelvis, more confidence in stepping without the arms being straight out in front of the body, and some sense of where it's safe to step, advice that is readily offered by the parent doing the supporting. So these are important lessons.

God is the parent who patiently holds our hands as we learn to "ambulate" along our own spiritual path. When your own back is getting stiff from leaning over an infant, remember that God leans endlessly over us, awaiting the moment when we can "mount up with wings as eagles" (Isaiah 40:31, KJV).

So walk tall, pilgrim! Take bold steps in the hands of God, and delight in those steps along the way.

Come to the feast!

Your infant has been enjoying solid foods for several months now, but the eleventh-month baby brings that enjoyment to a high art. Have you noticed your baby picking up a handful of baby-food squash or applesauce and smearing it into his hair? He is making himself a participant in all steps of the process, whether parents see him as a participant or not!

Babies love finger foods. This probably has several reasons. (Doesn't everything about human behavior seem to have multiple reasons?) The infant enjoys being a part of the process, as we said. He enjoys the sensory input of the feel of the food; he also revels in the manual dexterity it takes to actually get the food into the mouth, although he's been practicing this maneuver for several months. Finally, he experiences a sense of control as he decides what, when, and how much food goes into his mouth. Even in the first year of life, humans love control.

Each different taste and texture has to be learned. The muscles of the tongue, palate, and pharynx, which have begun a complex series of manipulations for purposes of articulating words, can be brought into use by the infant as he learns how to swallow a liquid, a cracker, a cooked potato, a carrot stick. Swallowing is not a single or a simple skill. The texture, viscosity, and temperature of a food substance will all play a role in how the muscles of the mouth are used to swallow that food. The baby learns important information about all three of those traits of the food by manipulating the food with the hands before taking a bite.

Of course, if the eleventh-month child has teeth (normal teething begins anywhere from three to twelve months of age, so he may or may not have any yet), they will help with the eating of hard or crunchy foods. If not, the tongue and muscles of the mouth will help the child "gum" the substance and soften the food using saliva (of which the child has no lack, I am certain).

God gives each of us "finger foods" at different times in our spiritual lives. These are to help us make the transition from milk to solid foods, from infancy to maturity in our Christian life, as the writer of Hebrews mentions (5:11-14). I believe that God does this "finger feeding" of spiritual transition foods with us for much the same reasons that the infant enjoys finger feeding himself now. We each enjoy being participants in the process of our own spiritual development—in fact, if we didn't participate actively, we wouldn't feel that it was truly *ours*. God sends us physical tokens—"transition foods," in a sense—to connect us with our heavenly Parent. A sermon that speaks to us forcefully and personally, a life-changing encounter, even a quiet walk in the woods—these are bridges to the Almighty.

In worship, we call a physical token of God a sacrament, something real and enfleshed that points to God, and so it is when we take the cup and eat the bread of the Lord's Supper. Jesus said, "I am the living bread that came down from heaven. Whoever eats of this bread will live forever; and the bread that I will give for the life of the world is my flesh" (John 6:50-51, NRSV). Whether we believe that the eucharistic bread becomes the actual body of Christ, or whether we believe it is a symbol of Christ's sacrifice for us, the goal is the same: oneness with Christ. The Communion liturgy invites us to come to the "joyful feast of the Lord"—sometime, watch your baby's "joyful feast," and consider what it means to be nourished by the Bread of Life.

Why isn't my baby talking yet?

The eleventh-month baby's babble has been incessant for months now. Probably in that time you have heard him come up with at least one sound that approximated a real word. In this month you're likely to hear three or four new words emerge from your child's talented mouth! You may hear something like "Mama" and "Dada"; perhaps there's a word for a sibling, or "buh-buh" for bottle, or a "duh-duh" for the family dog. (I find that many children's first word is the family dog's name. They probably hear it as frequently as any other word, with the possible exception of no!).

The child will enjoy showing off his mastery of these two

or more words. Sometimes he may chant the words over and over, as if to practice their articulation, so parents may think he's requesting a bottle because he says "buh-buh," and then they are mystified that he throws it away when they give it to him! He's merely playing with the word (but don't doubt that he logged the fact that when he said the word, *you* gave him the bottle). He may delight in going back and forth between the words in his vocabulary, just for fun.

A word of caution here: don't be alarmed if a child you know has no words yet, or if a child has a vocabulary of twenty-five. Word acquisition among infants varies greatly, mediated by several factors. There may be a genetic component—I find that a late talker might have a parent who was also a late talker. The timing of an infant's word acquisition will also be influenced by his learning style—if he is an auditory learner, he will have more words at this stage than if he is primarily a kinesthetic learner. Sometimes, too, a child may just choose not to work on talking! He'll concentrate on other things instead and catch up on the words later.

Birth order makes a difference, too. The first-born child has two doting adults (usually) to talk to him for most of the day, and the background environment is fairly calm. These children tend to be intense and focus for long periods of time on one endeavor; they can be a little bit introverted; and they learn words early because words are the "currency" of their parents' world. First-borns tend to go into careers such as law and medicine: ninety percent of my medical school class were first-borns. The second-born child, however, has two more-harried adults trying to give him care, with less time for verbal input. Meanwhile there's a two-, three-, or four-year-old sibling racing around in the background, making noise and moving fast. Second-borns tend to be more outgoing and

even-keeled in the first year of life and then strongly opinion-
ated in the second year of life; they are oriented almost
entirely to the acquisition of motor skills (they are the climb-
ers and jumpers who go on to be the professional athletes)
because they are goaded by the skills of the older sibling. And
they are later talkers because the older sibling interprets for
them and because they are putting all their mental energies
into motor activities.

For a more complete exploration of this interesting subject,
read *The Birth Order Book* by Kevin Leman. I happen to think
it's valuable information for parents, not so much to determine
"who this child will be," but because we tend to parent out of
our own birth-order characteristics and to emotionally affiliate
most closely with our child in the same birth-order position as
we were. Sometimes an awareness of that can help problem-
atic family dynamics tremendously!

The take-home message here, as I tell parents, is that an
infant will acquire words at his own rate. If you have concerns
about that issue, talk with your pediatrician or health-care
provider about it. Chances are good that your child is within
normal limits and just has his own marvelous sense of timing!

As you watch any infant acquire discrete words, remember
that God is waiting, always, for us to learn to think in, and to
speak, the language of joy and grace and obedience. Each of
us may express this language in different ways; each of us
may develop these "spiritual skills" under a different timetable—but God welcomes each of us as sisters and brothers in
the family of Christ.

Screeech!

Has your eleven-month-old gotten noisy lately?

Believe it or not, he may be trying to get your attention—even though he's pretty much been the center of your universe for more than a year now, if you include pregnancy. He apparently feels that he should be the focus of your awareness every moment and that if you are not talking or playing with him, you're simply not doing your job. A lot of babies around this age try to get their parents' attention by screeching.

Actually, he's probably figured out by now that screeching gets the attention of all adults in a room, on an airplane, or at the park. But what the baby really hopes to do is to get *his parents'* attention, not that of other peripheral adults. He has also figured out that if parents are actively engaged in conversation with another adult, and he screeches long and loud enough, he will get his parents to stop the other conversation and perhaps even carry him away from the other adults, in this way ensuring Mom and Dad's undivided attention. In other words, he is competing with anyone else Mom or Dad might be talking to.

This is even effective during a worship service. Did you ever notice that when infants begin to fuss, screech, or in some other way disrupt the worship service for their parents, it's often during the sermon? That may be because the baby is tired or because the little darling feels the need to compete with that loud person up front. (Not that this information will make any difference in how the worship services actually go for parents in the next twelve months, but I thought you'd like to know at least one reason it happens.) And please keep in mind that, whatever the reason for the screaming, it's a kindness to fellow worshipers to remove a screaming infant from a worship setting!

Some of us have been known to screech pretty loudly when we think God is ignoring us. We want God's attention, and we want it NOW. But, just as the eleven-month-old doesn't understand that he will always have his parents' attention, even if Mom or Dad isn't physically looking at him and hanging on to his every word, so we don't always realize that we will always have God's attention.

Just maybe, if we stopped screeching for a little while, we might be able to hear the voice of Love trying to get through to us.

Chapter 12

First Steps . . . Maybe: The Twelfth Month

You've watched your baby learn to pull to a stand; you've seen her become adept at cruising the furniture; you've helped her walk "hand in hand" with you. Now, watch carefully as your baby makes her way around the couch or coffee table, and you'll probably see her stand unaided for anywhere from ten seconds to two minutes. This is a prelude to that all-important First Step. This unsupported standing helps her strengthen the quadriceps muscle, practice locking the knee and the ankle, and work at balancing the torso quite nicely on the pelvis and legs.

Walking is not an easy task—ask anyone who has been injured in a car accident, who has suffered a stroke, or who has endured a prolonged convalescence off the feet. These folks have had to learn to walk all over again, and it is not as simple as you might think. Walking in a coordinated fashion involves picking up a foot, swinging it through an arc to plant the heel in front of the walker, then rolling the weight from heel to toe on that foot, and, while balancing the weight on the ball of that foot, beginning the process with the foot on the opposite side. Meanwhile, the arms and hands are swinging on the contralateral (opposite) side, for balance—the idea being to keep the torso balanced over the pelvis. This is all done in a fluid series of movements that also serve to preserve momentum and propel the walker in a forward direction.

A baby learning to take a first step has no sense of the arm movement at all and no understanding of the arc-like movement made by the lower legs and feet. The baby awkwardly picks up one foot and plants the entire foot on the floor, then attempts to regain her balance before repeating the process on the other side, so as to make forward progress. Over weeks, the infant will learn the fluid and coordinated motions between arms and legs that characterize the more adult-looking gait. For every time the baby makes a successful foot plant and stays vertical, there will be three or four times where she takes a tumble and sits down—rather forcefully!

You'll notice your baby doing the "look, Ma, no hands!" trick for longer and longer periods. When the baby is standing without using hands for 90–120 seconds, the first step will occur. As you can imagine, this activity is a well-orchestrated symphony of peripheral nerves and CNS working together, along with the sense of balance and proprioception. The end result? Approximately one week after an infant's first step, she will be walking across the room pretty well. I do remind parents from time to time, "Don't be concerned if she tries the walking thing for a few days and then reverts to a crawl once more; she's merely being pragmatic for the moment. She knows how to get places by crawling, and it's still risky to try this new walking movement. Don't worry. She'll be intrigued enough with this new (and adult) mode of locomotion to go back to it in another week or so." No baby, offered the option of walking as adults do, will continue to crawl for longer than a month or so!

You say *your* baby isn't walking yet and isn't even showing any signs in that direction? As with many of the other motor skills, there is a big variation in timing. Some infants walk at eight months (a few, amazingly, earlier); the majority learn between ten and thirteen months of age; and a very few will take even longer to walk. There is a hint of an indirect correlation with intelligence in some cases: Einstein supposedly walked at seventeen months, Thomas Edison at fifteen months. I often need to remind both parents and grandparents, "Be patient. Toddlers are hard to catch, and you have plenty of time to be running after your toddler, so relax! She'll get to it when she gets to it."

God is the awesome God who created the central nervous system, the intricate muscle, tendon, and ligament system of upper and lower extremities, and some joints that are true works of art in three dimensions. These have learned, in the time frame of twelve months, to go all the way from absolute physical helplessness to independent walking! Not only that, but the child can perceive the environment around her, decide which direction to go, and just *go*.

God gives us the "terrible gift" (as Madeleine L'Engle calls it in *Walking on Water)* of free will. Each one of us, as humans, is able to choose of our own free will which directions we will go in life. Will we go forward or backward? Left or right? Make a good or bad decision? Will we choose selfishness or service to others? Will we find joyful living in the shadow of God's eternal Spirit, or depressed and anxious living, believing that we are valued only for what we can do, never for who we are? Will each of us embrace unconditional love, or will we turn down the free gift of (amazing!) grace?

I wonder what God feels while watching each of us learn to walk along our spiritual journey. After all, a twelfth-month child's choices are kitchen or living room, not ultimate life or ultimate death. To walk humbly with God is the best choice, so Micah tells us: "And what does the Lord require of you? To act justly and to love mercy and to walk humbly with your God" (Mic. 6:8).

Infant delight and divine applause

One of the more delightful games a twelfth-month infant enjoys at this time of life is the "clap hands" game. She will clap hands together in imitation of what the parents do. For that matter, she'll even clap hands with an adult other than her parents, as long as Mom or Dad is close by. It's actually a kind of shorthand for friendship and good will and could be thought of as the twelve-month-old's equivalent of a handshake.

Of course, at the beginning, the baby doesn't associate any emotions with the clapping of hands; it's only a skill to be practiced. But as she sees parents say, "yay, good job!" and clap *their* hands while smiling, she will learn to associate it with the message "you did something right" or "congratulations!" Babies love to be cheered, as anyone could notice, and a parent could talk the baby into almost anything at this time by clapping the hands in congratulations. Babies pretty quickly learn to associate smiles and even laughter with the clapping of hands.

And most certainly, infants have no pride about such things. They are more than willing to applaud themselves quickly and thoroughly for almost any accomplishment. They will often hesitate before attempting something, and look expectantly at a parent, waiting to see if the parent will applaud even the attempt. They look to adults for a sign of approval of the action, whatever it might be. A delighted twelve-month-old infant, laughing and clapping for herself, must delight the heart of God, as she delights the hearts of most human beings.

How good are we at clapping for ourselves? Somewhere along the line, in later childhood, we learn to applaud for someone else's achievement. After the preschool Christmas play, the audience applauds the players. At the children's theater production, we applaud the actors and musicians. In Sunday school classes, we hear children applaud after the storyteller has given the tale. By the age of five, most children will not applaud themselves any longer. They have learned that applause is something reserved for those (others) who have "performed" and that the expected response of the spectators of the performance is applause. No wonder people in worship services sometimes agonize over whether to applaud a beautiful cantata, a gorgeous Bach prelude well executed on the organ, a lovely original musical composition of praise music, even a great sermon. We have been conditioned that applause is a "secular" activity that interrupts worship and is therefore inappropriate in a worship service.

I believe that twelve-month-olds are teaching us that applause very much belongs in worship. After all, in the worship setting, the audience is not the congregation; the audience is God, and *all* the congregation are the worshipers, the "players." Scripture after Scripture describes those who worship praising God with the clapping of hands (reread Psalm 100, for instance). We can most certainly worship by clapping our hands—it's not a disruption of worship but an integral part! So, as we clap for a beautiful solo sung, after a wonderful clarinet piece, or following a grand and glorious reading of Scripture, are we not praising God for that person's gifts?

One could as easily applaud God on a mountaintop while gazing at fields of wildflowers, or at the ocean watching the great whales at play.

But I think there is a deeper message from the twelve-month-old infant. Notice that the infant applauds *herself* and her own accomplishments. Adults have forgotten how to do that entirely. The baby is delighted with something she's done, and she applauds, expecting parents to do likewise. She is able to take pride in her own achievements, and she looks to the parents for approval, as well.

But can most of us say the same, that we take pride in our own achievements? In my experience, no. Many of us struggle with feeling as if we don't measure up. I think it comes from the messages all around us that we are valued for what we achieve.

Society tells us this in so many ways. We're graded at school from an early age; six-year-olds give each other scores on the playground for the best cartwheel, the best jump, the best monkey-bar climb; teenagers have gotten the message that they're only as acceptable as their wardrobe; executives in the workplace buy into the dog-eat-dog ethic early or do not survive. And then along comes the twelve-month-old to remind us that God applauds us!

God does not value us for what we do, but for who we are. The mere fact of our existence makes us valuable to God—as Thomas Aquinas said, "[God] loves each of us as if there were only one of us." The entire message of the Good News is that we are so valuable to God that the Creator arranged for our mistakes and shortcomings to be, in effect, "canceled out," and came to earth in human form to ensure that we could spend eternity with the author of Love. If that doesn't emphasize our value, then nothing does.

And if we are that valuable to the Creator of the universe, and our worth has nothing to do with our accomplishments, then we can be applauded merely for *be*ing. Our delight in ourselves can transcend any "ego" needs that we have, because that delight and the congratulations that accompany that delight really go back to God. We can applaud ourselves, not because we have a need to be applauded (that need means that we still value ourselves, and others, for what we *do*), but because we are God's creation and we are valued for that reason. And so it ought to become easier, within the church, to applaud each other as valued objects of God's unending Love and to applaud ourselves as one of those valued objects.

Let the unselfconsciousness of an infant's applause remind you that the Good News is really very simple, and yet it is worth everything we have, everything we are, everything we can hope to be. Your worth has nothing to do with this crazy, mixed-up world and its crazy, mixed-up values. Your worth has everything to do with the sun, moon, and stars, with the mountains and the oceans, with the beasts of the fields and the birds of the air—all of these are interconnected, and we are connected to all of them by the creative power of God, who knows and loves you more deeply than you can ever know and love yourself. Now that's worth clapping about!

The in and out game

The twelve-month-old infant plays a number of exploring games, and play is more focused, lasts longer, and is perhaps a bit messier than most parents had anticipated. But this is how babies must learn, and so adults must learn to put up with a certain amount of mess. One of the main themes of play now is what I call "the in and out game."

The baby will now explore taking things *out*, in all kinds of ways. The kitchen drawer is opened, and everything is taken out and dumped on the floor. The laundry basket is emptied, again onto the floor! Blocks are dumped out of their container and onto the floor. (A container with safe edges and a few blocks make a fascinating toy for the baby now.) She may put the blocks back into the container and dump them out, over and over again. The baby seems to delight in taking things out of other things—such as the dishwasher or the clothes dryer. Parents can easily trace the path of their baby around the house by following the piles of objects on the floor!

But the other part of the game is the *in* part. And babies usually use themselves as the object to be put in, before they use other objects. A twelve-month baby will try to put herself into the dishwasher or the clothes dryer. She will put herself in the little space between the sofa and the wall. She will put herself into the space under the kitchen or dining-room table, even into the drawer she has just emptied of its more mundane contents. And then what does she do? She turns around and laughs.

Developmental specialists tell us that the twelfth-month infant is beginning to explore the relationship between two objects. They call this the "preposition" phase: what does it mean for something to be "over" something else? Under? Around? Inside? Beside? So she begins with "what does it mean for my body to be *in* a small space?" and a bit later will investigate the possible relationships between two objects. We could say to ourselves, "That's pretty concrete thinking," and leave it at that, if it weren't for that laugh.

The baby may laugh because she's happy to have achieved the goal she set out to achieve—getting into the small space under the coffee table. But why does she choose such small, confined spaces? I think it's one of God's delightful little jokes, built into the sequence of human development: the baby laughs because she realizes that she can get into the small, confined space and that adults cannot. Think of this: your child has lived for almost a year now, watching all of the amazing things you, the parents, know how to do. On every conceivable front, you excel. You can walk, you can talk, you can manipulate objects, you can read books and magazines, you talk to your friends, drive a car to get to places you wish to go, exchange money for things you want, decide where and how you will spend your time, and determine what and when you will eat. The infant can do none of those things at the beginning of life. She is only now starting to do a few of them, and not well at that.

But this one thing she *can* do better than Mom or Dad! She can crawl into a small, tight-fitting place and be comfortable there. She realizes on some cognitive level that parents cannot fit into a small space, because they're too big (once again, the relationship of two objects!). And this is the one circumstance where parents have to pay the price for their bigness and their abilities to control the whole world (or what seems to the baby to be the whole world). This is her one chance for real control, and she takes it, laughing with delight at the thought!

Up until now, parents have not seen their baby laugh over too many of the accomplished milestones but this one seems to delight the child. This is apparently some kind of delightful "hiccup" in developmental progression—the child places value on being able to get into small spaces, in a different way from the value she placed on being able to chew her own toes. It is, literally, a chance for the baby to laugh at the parents after all these months. I believe God built this into infants so that parents would remember the gift of humility. (I do mention to parents, "Be warned—the gift of humility will be seen again in your child's second year of life! Get comfortable with it now, because you will have many chances to be familiar with it in the coming year.")

Of course, when you reflect on the past year, it can make

you feel very humbled. No one could have told you ahead of time all the ways in which you would be stretched as a parent in this first year of your child's life. You've learned many things, both about your child and about yourself, in these remarkable twelve months. My hope is that this book will have helped you learn both about your baby and about God along the way.

Jesus was a toddler, too

We are coming to the close of this book in which we have traced an infant's accomplishments in the first year of life. But we are far from the end of the story! Now you will move into a new phase, as the parent of a toddler—may God be with you! You'll continue to see your baby gain motor, language, and social skills at a great rate. She'll learn something new every day—and so, probably, will you.

Raising a toddler has its joys and its trials, just as everything else in life has joys and trials. I tell the parents of my twelve-month-old patients, "You will have some sleepless nights, but you are used to that by now. You will have to remember to keep your sense of humor, as you have been practicing this past year. You will need to be careful of *you* sometimes, and your spouse, and make plans for a getaway every now and then. These are things you know. The things you don't know yet are too numerous to list here (perhaps some of them will deserve a book of their own someday). The joys of constant discovery, of affection given and received, of your child's first 'I love you' await you in the future. You will never be bored in your role as parent—how many other endeavors can promise that?"

Many people characterize the toddler phase as "terrible"—I

don't believe that, but it is a period of time in which high energy levels are required of parents, so I caution parents to sleep when they can. One thought that I think helps Christian parents along the way is to remember that Jesus was a toddler, too. This means that he climbed the pantry shelves when he wasn't supposed to; he delighted in running the other way when Mary called him to dinner; he solemnly shook his head no while touching Joseph's saw collection in the carpenter shop, even though he had been warned not to touch them. These were not sins on his part. They were normal explorations of the limits of his world. Jesus, as a toddler, pushed the limits, just as any toddler will, and he learned from his mistakes, just as every child will.

A toddler is not inherently evil in the way a few parents in my practice have tried to tell me. But it may be a difficult time for many parents because the child is testing all the limits all the time, and it takes energy to stand firm in those limits. It's much easier for a parent to give in when a child has been screaming for a cookie for the past ten minutes, than to hold firm to the "no cookies before dinner" rule. But if there is value in the "no cookies before dinner" rule (and I, as a pediatrician, think there is), then all children need to learn that one. The boy Jesus had to learn "no cookies before dinner" also, and no climbing the pantry shelves, and no touching the saws in the carpenter shop without supervision.

It's all a part of God's marvelous design for human development. That sequence of human development (the same regardless of culture, race, language group, or geography) is one of the bonds that connect us, as humans, to each other. It is one of the bonds that connect us, as Christians, to our God—for God, in the form of Jesus Christ, experienced all of these stages, too.

"So," I tell the parents in my practice, "if there is a time in the next year when you feel frustrated with your child's behavior, try to see the humor in God's dilemma of toddler development: the God who created stars and galaxies, plants and animals, time and space, and the God who loves you more than you can possibly imagine, was told to get off the kitchen table, mind his manners with company, and wash his hands before dinner! That should at least put a smile on your face once in awhile."

Chapter 13

On with the Journey!

Congratulations—your baby is a year old! This must feel like a tremendous milestone, and it is. You, his parents, have brought him through, healthy (most of the time), happy, and growing in so many wonderful ways. You sacrificed time, money, and sleep for the sake of your baby. And, as you look at your baby (who now may actually be "your toddler," if he's walking), you forget all the sleepness nights and labor pains and the body that won't quite get back to pre-baby shape, and you know: It was worth it all. This child is worth it all. And the God who brought your baby to you brought you all through.

My prayer is that, through this book and through watching, living with, and enjoying your baby, you've been able to come a little closer to that God. I hope that the "infant theology" we've been exploring has helped you discover a God who cherishes and encourages our continued growth and learning; a God who understands that we, the created, are "works in progress"; a God who delights in surprising us; a God of celebration.

Remember the deep joy you felt when you first heard your baby laugh? Recall the wonders of your infant lifting his head, clapping his hands, waving bye-bye, sprouting a first tooth, saying a first word, and (maybe) taking a first step. Any child's life is a celebration of the creativity of God—that child's ability to create, to imagine, to play is a celebration of God's creativity, imagination, and love of play. The child will continue to cocreate with God through the next several years and, I hope, through a lifetime, because the love of God calls us to cocreate life. That is the nature of love: it calls forth life. Your child knows that now—may he never forget.

We've also seen how all the different abilities work together and build on each other: the small motor skills enhance the language skills enhance the social skills that enhance the large motor skills . . . and on and on. This is a wonderful metaphor for the church, which the apostle Paul likened to a single body, with eyes and hands and heart and lungs. All gifts are needed in the realm of God!

As you reflect on your baby's achievements, remember, too, that your baby isn't the only special person in your house! God loves you and celebrates who you are. My hope is that you can continue to show your children that living in the love of God, incarnate in Christ, is the only way to life abundant. (Praying with your baby is a good habit to get into now. It will serve you well in your role as parent in the years ahead.) Madeleine L'Engle calls the Incarnation "the glorious impossible." God cared enough about us to come to Earth, live among us, die for us, and live again for us—inviting us to trust in the Son and therefore spend eternity in the presence of Love. By sharing and rejoicing in that "glorious impossible" with your child—or any child—you will help him or her to be the best person, the best reflection of God's love and joy, that child was created to be. And isn't that really what parenting is all about?

soli Deo gloria